THE ECONOMY OF THE SOUL

*Making World-Changing Investments
without Fear*

M.A. Hayward

WestBow
PRESS
A DIVISION OF THOMAS NELSON

WestBow Press books may be ordered through booksellers or by contacting:

WestBow Press
A Division of Thomas Nelson
1663 Liberty Drive
Bloomington, IN 47403
www.westbowpress.com
1-(866) 928-1240

ISBN: 978-1-4497-1725-4 (sc)
ISBN: 978-1-4497-1727-8 (hc)
ISBN: 978-1-4497-1726-1 (e)

Library of Congress Control Number: 2011929062

Author photo photo credit: Fran Russell
Editor: Anne Marie Petty
Scripture taken from the HOLY BIBLE, NEW INTERNATIONAL VERSION®. Copyright © 1973, 1978, 1984 by International Bible Society. Used by permission of Zondervan Publishing House. All rights reserved.
Printed in the United States of America

WestBow Press rev. date: 5/23/2011

CONTENTS

ACKNOWLEDGMENTS

Thank you, first and foremost, to God my Savior for the life, purpose, and place you have given me in your kingdom and family. You always seem to lead me places I feel I have no place going. Thank you also to my wife, Patricia, for your support, encouragement, and partnership. It is not good for me to be alone, so God has given me you. Thank you to my kids, Devin and Victoria, for being such good sports. It is an honor and a privilege to watch you grow. I learn so much through you. Thank you to my parents, Ralph and Judy, whose encouragement and generous support have greatly helped this effort along. Thank you for seeing and trusting the work God is doing in and through me. And thank you also to my high family – the saints of Faith Community Church of Rohnert Park. Thank you for walking with me and sharing your lives with me. I am so richly blessed.

Thank you; specifically; to my editor; long time friend; and sister in Christ Anne Marie; you have saved many semi-colons from wasteful misuse; and perhaps shameful abuse.

I am thankful for my "partners in crime;" my fellow shepherds: Ben Cunningham of Calvary Community, Dave Gould from Mt. Gilead, George Russell from New Hope, Dr. Bill Wagner with Snyder Lane Baptist, and Phil Jennings from Gateway. Your prayerful support and partnership in the Gospel are of immeasurable value.

Thank you to the faculty at Golden Gate Baptist Theological Seminary. Dr. Celum, Dr. Durst, Dr. Gainey, Dr. Gautsch, Dr. Higgs, Dr. Iorg, Dr. McCoy, the Drs. Melick, Dr. Robertson, Dr.

Shouse, Dr. Thompson, and Dr. Wagner, your love for God and your passion for the knowledge and grace of Christ are evident. Your many investments are yielding a return. This isn't for a grade, but I hope you are able to enjoy it.

I also want to thank those mentors who don't know me from a hole in the ground and have no idea how they have impacted my life, ministry, and message: Charles Stanley, Chip Ingram, Chuck Swindoll, Erwin McManus, Francis Chan, Greg Laurie, Henry Blackaby, and John Eldridge. You have all been used by God to touch many more lives than you can know in this life.

To God be all glory, honor, and praise. Amen.

Why Should I Even Read This?

—

Our most valuable commodity is our time. No matter how wisely we invest our time, we can never earn more. Therefore, it is wise to discern whether an opportunity is worthwhile, or a waste of our precious time.

If you are attending church, you are wasting your time. Church attendance has never been the purpose of Christ's coming. We waste so much time trying to develop strategies to "get people to church" that we completely miss the whole point of our redemption. In fact, mere church attendance can be a hindrance to becoming all God called you to be.

If we remain content with committing an hour, or two, of our week to church attendance, then that time is not well spent. A good investment is one that yields a return. Though we cannot earn more time, we can get a good return for the investment of our time. We cannot merely attend church and expect to see that return. We need to *be* the church. We cannot try to get people to church, we need to draw people to Christ and help them *become* the church.

Our culture functions within the dynamic of give and take, within an economy. We want to know if an investment is worth the cost and instantly ask the question, "What's in it for me?" As long as we are asking that question, we are not in a right relationship with God and cannot make an impact in this world for Christ; we are still lost in self. The Bible teaches us that we need to die to self. We need to change our thinking, be "transformed by the renewing of our minds" (Romans 12:2). We need to trade in this self-centered economy based on "me" for a greater, Kingdom economy based on our love for and trust in Christ. We need to ask, "What's in it for him?"

Why do you need to read this? Because, if you are still just "attending church," you don't get it. You are reconciled to God to be reconciled to his people and be an active part of his church and its mission, not just attend it. All your struggles, failures, victories, and lessons learned are not just for you; they are for the edification of those around you. This book is here for *you*. My life is here for *you*. I've suffered, struggled, and overcome for *you*. You need to read this because God has something to say to *you*. Maybe you've heard the message twenty times already, but God wants you to "get it." Knowing *about* God and the life he has called you to is vastly different than *knowing* it.

The Prospectus and the Payoff

—

Your life is not what it was meant to be. You don't need me to tell you that. Our insatiable longing for more tells us that. The fact is that we were made for eternal glory but live in temporal decay. If we are not aware of the origin of the longing, it can quickly turn into greed, lust, and selfish materialism. You want more because you were made for more, but you need more of the right thing – a pure desire, not a selfish desire.

More begins with purpose. It is the big question for everyone who embarks on a life of faith. "Okay, God has a plan for my life. So what is his will? What is my purpose?" Authors like Pastor Rick Warren have many very good things to say on that, but let me boil it down to something travel-sized: Your purpose is to know God and make God known. That is why you are made in his image and nothing else in creation is. Think about it, everything in the physical universe is made of the same basic materials, yet we even differ from other primates by 2%. The distinction is not only physical. It is no wonder that we can train gorillas to use sign language, but how come they can't seem to teach us their language?

We were created in the image of God so we could relate to him and connect with him. Because of that unique relationship, God gave mankind dominion and authority over the rest of creation. We have a moral compass (whether we use it or not). You never see tigers getting put in tiger prison for eating their young because there is no right or wrong there. We, however lock murderers away for life sentences.

We are creative. We have a veritable buffet of emotions. We have free will. These are all gifts from our Creator. All animals have a "spirit," defined as an independent will of their own, but they do not have a soul; that part of us which is created in God's image to allow us to know him and relate to him on various levels and reflect him.

There are those who are atheist, meaning they are opposed to thoughts of God. It does not mean they don't have such thoughts, only that they are opposed to them. These can be divided into two categories: 1) Those who think all that is came about by random chance, and 2) those who think aliens are responsible for life as we know it (which begs the question, where did *they* come from?). Neither of these really have a leg to stand on because random chance is a mathematical impossibility, and alien intervention requires far more faith than the acknowledgement of a divine Creator. Atheism, in a very real way, is just another religion where mankind, and his ability to reason, is held up in the place of God.

Apart from atheism, there are a myriad of world religions that stand as evidence of mankind's spiritual component. People of every tribe and tongue and nation have a very real sense that there is more to life than what is understood through the five senses. Each of these cultures is on a quest to make sense of that longing, find the meaning of life, and receive what they have determined to be "eternal reward."

All this is to say that deep in each of us is a longing for significance, meaning, and purpose. To know God is to be filled by him. We are filled by him in order that we can pour out – invest in others. We want more than an "everyday life," but we don't want to pay too much to get it. We know, in the depths of our heart, that there is more, but we are afraid of what "more" will cost. So why is more so hard to find? Why are so many – even in the church – lost in existence and longing for life?

In Luke chapter sixteen, Jesus tells a parable that will help us answer that question. It is the only parable where one of the characters is actually given a name. Some hold that this might indicate it has its foundation in an actual occurrence. It is the parable of the rich man and Lazarus.

> "There was a rich man who was dressed in purple and fine linen and lived in luxury every day. At his gate was laid a beggar named Lazarus, covered with sores and longing to eat what fell from the rich man's table. Even the dogs came and licked his sores. The time came when the beggar died and the angels carried him to Abraham's side. The rich man also died and was buried. In hell, where he

was in torment, he looked up and saw Abraham far away, with Lazarus by his side. So he called to him, 'Father Abraham, have pity on me and send Lazarus to dip the tip of his finger in water and cool my tongue, because I am in agony in this fire.'

But Abraham replied, 'Son, remember that in your lifetime you received your good things, while Lazarus received bad things, but now he is comforted here and you are in agony. And besides all this, between us and you a great chasm has been fixed, so that those who want to go from here to you cannot, nor can anyone cross over from there to us.'

He answered, 'Then I beg you, father, send Lazarus to my father's house, for I have five brothers. Let him warn them, so that they will not also come to this place of torment.'

Abraham replied, 'They have Moses and the Prophets; let them listen to them.'

'No, father Abraham,' he said, 'but if someone from the dead goes to them, they will repent.'

He said to him, 'If they do not listen to Moses and the Prophets, they will not be convinced even if someone rises from the dead.'"

~ Luke 16:19-31

As the rich man lived a "nice little life" of comfort and ease he remained blissfully unaware of, or moved by, the desperate need lying right outside his own front door. While the man enjoyed the excessive luxury and comfort of expensive and rare purple robes, Lazarus simply, humbly, longed for even the wasted crumbs that fell to the floor from the rich man's table. How easy would it have been to give the poor beggar some bread? Send a servant out to toss him a left-over. The mindset of Jesus' day was that blessings come from God to the righteous and faithful while hardship, disease, and poverty are given by God to the sinful. The rich man was not a bad man. He went to synagogue, obeyed the food laws, tithed his income, and brought his sacrifice to the temple. He faithfully "attended church." He was not legally obligated to help Lazarus; at least not by the *letter* of the Law.

On the other hand, Lazarus, the poor beggar, was not only impoverished and paralyzed, but was also riddled with sores and going hungry. Day after day he would lie exposed to the elements in the hopes that someone would show some mercy and compassion. Could you imagine your life being completely dependent upon the compassion and generosity of others? Most of us would rather be marooned on an island by pirates. At least then you get a pistol with one shot.

When Lazarus dies, he is escorted by angels into the presence of his "father" Abraham. By virtue of his reception, we know that Lazarus was not a rank sinner afflicted for his shame; rather, in spite of his poverty and affliction, he remained right with God. How easy would it have been for Lazarus to judge God based on his circumstances and turn away? What Lazarus received in eternity for his faithful perseverance far outweighed his temporal suffering.

We are not told how much time elapsed between the death of Lazarus and the death of the rich man. No doubt, when Lazarus died, any burden the rich man carried because of his presence was lifted.

In 2003, my wife and I bought the house we now live in with the intent of having her dad move in with us. Greg suffered from Multiple Sclerosis and it had advanced to a place where he needed extra help in his daily routines. We knew when we made the living arrangements that this would be a growing commitment. At first, Greg was still fairly mobile and independent. About three years into his stay, he developed an infection that went unnoticed and became systemic. While in the hospital being treated, he suffered a mild stroke, which further disabled him. Life just got much more challenging. Though we were committed to care for him in the home once he was able to leave the hospital, I was terrified. How much more would I have to give? Did I have what it would take? Would I even be willing to make the investment when the time came to up the ante?

Greg lived nearly three more years and died in September of 2008. We were grieved to lose him. Both of my wife's parents were now gone. Greg, in spite of all his struggles and losses, was a man of faith and joy. He spread that joy everywhere he went as he gave testimony to the faithfulness and provision of God. As hard as it was to watch him die, there was also a sense of relief. His suffering was over, and a very difficult season of our own lives had come to a close. It may sound insensitive, but there is no use denying that sense of relief. For those who have the hope of eternal life, physical death is not the end and that concept is easier to come to peace with. It was a joy to serve Greg, and God used that season to bring about so much good, far beyond my own life. It was still, in many ways, a burden.

The rich man in Jesus' parable had no such grief when Lazarus passed; only relief. When we set our sights, desires, and hopes on the temporal and seek to build a nice little life for ourselves, every investment, every act of kindness, compassion, and generosity becomes a burden. I have to confess, there were times when the last thing I wanted to do was serve Greg. There were days when I thought God was being horribly unfair and robbing me of my hopes and dreams and goals. There were days where I was more worried about me and my temporal expectations than God's eternal plan. Most likely the rich man felt great relief the day Lazarus didn't show up at his gate. That nagging reminder of his selfishness and greed – his wickedness – was now gone. He could go back to attending church without being challenged to actually *be* the church. Life gets so easy when we are not challenged in our thinking or made uncomfortable by being confronted with who we really are. Yet we need that, don't we?

Death is the one thing we cannot control. It touches every life. Once both men in the parable have reached their eternal destination, we see a very different picture. Lazarus enjoys comfort and rest on an eternal scale in the embrace of his "father" Abraham. The Jews viewed father Abraham much like we view St. Peter at the "pearly gates." Neither is necessarily accurate, but it is what we have to work with. The rich man, on the other hand, receives the sum of his nice little life. The reality we need to grasp is that there is a much bigger picture than here and now that we need to see. The rich man had church; Lazarus had God.

What strikes me about this part of the parable is the rich man's renewed concern for his brothers. Apparently, the man never urged his brothers to search out and live by the Law and the Prophets before, but now he wants Lazarus to go warn them about the eternal reality. He wants something big and miraculous to impact his brothers. The message he receives in return is that they have been given enough and they need to simply respond to what they have already been given.

As I look at my own Christian life, I want more. "Good enough" no longer is. One night as I prayed, I asked God with all my heart to reveal himself in a way that would instill a greater fear of God in me. I wanted to see him and his glory in a way I could not deny; a way that would shake me up and make it easy for me to fear God over man. What God did, in his grace and generosity, was lead me to this parable in Luke. I find that I want what Isaiah got, what Ezekiel got, what John got. I want the shock-and-awe campaign. If I could just see God's majesty and glory then I would find it easier to fear God and disregard the intimidation of the world. God's response to me was very much Abraham's response to the rich man in torment, "I've given you so much already." If we haven't learned to see and know and fear God through all that he has given us already then perhaps we don't really want to? No miracle will touch the hardened heart. Perhaps wanting a miracle and waiting for it is a method of avoidance. There are so many miracles before us each day, yet somehow we manage to miss them.

As vast as is the chasm between Lazarus in heaven and the rich man in hell, so it is between knowing we ought to want something and actually wanting it. Seeing God and gaining understanding will change everything and we can kiss our nice little life and our tidy Christianity goodbye. To actually live the life Jesus is leading us to and experience the power and presence of God would mean taking steps of faith into what we now fear and seek to avoid. It means letting go of what we are desperately (and often secretly) clinging to. Therefore, though we can easily convince ourselves that we are deeply spiritual if we simply attend church faithfully, we will find ourselves missing the mark when God reveals our true heart. Which are we more concerned with, living a nice little life attending church and looking spiritual, or pursuing life in Christ as we are filled by a vibrant relationship with God and investing in others for his kingdom?

Buying In

This book is not for everybody. It is a call to self-evaluation and examination. It is a look deep into the mirror of scripture and frankly, many of us will not like what we see. As God has been at work in my own life to refine me as gold in the fire, I have been trying to put the pieces and lessons together. As God works in my life, so will he work through me in the lives of those to whom I minister. This book is a trail guide, a journal, for the adventure that God is bringing me through and I offer it to the people of God in the hopes that more will chose to follow and draw nearer to God.

The calloused non-believer, the content believer, the lukewarm church, these will not see a need to open themselves up for evaluation and conviction. Nobody likes to be wrong. We all want to feel like we are okay, that all is well. The reality is that perfection does not lie on this side of the veil of death. Comfort and contentment were never goals set before us by God. In fact, it is into Jesus' passion – his suffering – that we are invited and called. To follow Jesus will cost you your life; not all in one check, but day by day, installment after installment, he will ask for all you have to give each day.

If you are content with your status quo, you can stop reading. If you insist that you are as much like Jesus as you will ever get, close the book. If, however, you are burdened with a sense that there is more, that the Christianity you know falls short, missing the mark of what is portrayed in scripture, then by all means keep reading. If you are convinced that the God of the Bible is the same yesterday, today, and forever, yet you wonder why it is so hard to see Him in your context, then you need to travel through these pages. What is set before you is the road that God has been leading me along as he develops me as an individual and as a part of a whole. He wants to do the same in you.

There are many truths in scripture specific to the individual, but there are yet more foundational truths in God's word that apply to us all. When these truths remain unapplied there is a breakdown. As we survey our country and culture, we can clearly see there has been a serious breakdown. Something is missing; something is wrong. It is written, "For it is time for judgment to begin with the family of God" (1 Peter 4:17). It starts with you because you have been given much. With much blessing and revelation comes much responsibility. You have taken the name of Christ, and not in vain if you strive to find the "more." Therefore, you are accountable to represent and reveal God to a wounded and hungry world. We need to represent him well, so that through us Christ may be made known and the world around us will find healing, hope, and purpose in him.

You need to read this for the same reason I needed to write it: because you need to make a difference. That is why you have been redeemed. Jesus said, "No one lights a lamp and places it under a bowl" (Matthew 5:15). God did not put his light in you to hide you away in safety. The church you attend is not a trophy case where you go to be on display. You have been saved unto a purpose, to be used for the greater good. You are a tool, a vessel in the hands of the Master. You are to be filled by him, and to invest in others for him. It is through you that the kingdom of God will grow. As Jesus said, "From the days of John the Baptist until now, the kingdom of heaven has been forcefully advancing, and forceful men lay hold of it" (Matthew 11:12). There is a cost to be paid and a battle to be fought. There are investments to be made in others – even those we do not feel deserve it or who we do not consider a worthwhile investment. We are not to judge people, we are to obey God's commands.

We are called to be "a kingdom of priests and a holy nation." Figuring out what that looks like in your life is a process, a journey. The road is narrow and can be very bumpy. Stay the course. Pray your way through each leg of the journey. Trust God and seek him at every step. In fact, stop now. Stop and pray that God would stand with you as he shows you who you are and who you are to become. Make the decision right now that you are going to stand firm on his grace, trust his heart, and persevere through your journey. Make the commitment ahead of time to be faithful with whatever is set before you. Then, take the next step.

Isaiah 3:10-15

—

Tell the righteous it will be well with them,

for they will enjoy the fruit of their deeds.

Woe to the wicked! Disaster is upon them!

They will be paid back for what their hands have
done.

Youths oppress my people,

women rule over them.

O my people, your guides lead you astray;

they turn you from the path.

The LORD takes his place in court;

he rises to judge the people.

The LORD enters into judgment

against the elders and leaders of his people:

"It is you who have ruined my vineyard;

the plunder from the poor is in your houses.

What do you mean by crushing my people

and grinding the faces of the poor?"

declares the Lord, the LORD Almighty.

Chapter 1

The Economy of Self

Missing the Mark

—

"Tell the righteous it will be well with them, for they will enjoy the fruit of their deeds. Woe to the wicked! Disaster is upon them! They will be paid back for what their hands have done."
~ Isaiah 3:10, 11

We like the concept of justice. We need it; we demand it. The righteous are rewarded and the wicked are punished. It comes so naturally to us. The question is, then, who defines the boundary between righteous and wicked? What standard is used to determined which side of that spectrum I fall on? There are some consistencies that transcend culture; for example, mutilating children is wrong. We all agree that such things are evil. There is much, however, that seems to be far more inconsistent, and not so much from culture to culture, but within the life of a single individual. We expect certain courtesies from others, yet are able to justify the absence of those same courtesies in our own lives. We are offended when one does not forgive us, but we withhold forgiveness from another on the basis of some unwritten exception. We live from a "me-first" perspective. We are self-centered, and we are missing the whole point and purpose of life.

Sin is an ugly word. Our culture hates that word, but it is actually a perfect descriptor. Sin is a Hebrew word. It is a term used in archery to tell the shooter, "You have missed the mark." In an archery tournament, the likelihood of a competitive archer to just miss – to "air-ball" so to speak – is slim to none. If an archer missed the target, it was usually because he was aiming at the wrong one.

I can remember the winter Olympics of 2004, in the biathlon, there was such a case. American skier Matt Emmons was in the lead for the gold medal and he simply needed to shoot his last target. The Associated Press reported in an ESPN.com article published August 22, 2004:

> ATHENS, Greece -- Matt Emmons was focusing on staying calm. He should have been focusing on the right target.
>
> Emmons fired at the wrong one with his final shot Sunday, a shocking mistake that cost the American a commanding lead in the Olympic 50-meter three-position rifle final and ruined his chance for a second gold medal.
>
> Leading by three points and needing only to get near the bull's-eye to win, Emmons fired at the target in lane three while shooting in lane two. When no score appeared, he gestured to officials that he thought there was some sort of error with his target.
>
> "When I shot the shot, everything felt fine," Emmons said. "On those targets, sometimes every once in a great while, it won't register. The shot just doesn't show up, so that's what I thought happened."
>
> He was wrong. Officials huddled before announcing that Emmons had cross-fired -- an extremely rare mistake in elite competition -- and awarded him a score of zero. That dropped Emmons to eighth place

at 1,257.4 points and lifted Jia Zhanbo of China to the gold at 1,264.5.

When we miss the mark – when we sin – we are disqualified. No door-prize, no "close enough;" there is nothing. As we look around our world, our economy of self is leading us to just such a fate: nothing. Jesus gave this example:

> "The kingdom of heaven is like a king who prepared a wedding banquet for his son. He sent his servants to those who he had invited to the banquet to tell them to come, but they refused to come...Then he said to his servants, 'The wedding banquet is ready, but those I invited did not deserve to come. Go to the street corners and invite anyone you find.' So the servants went out and gathered all the people they could find, both good and bad, and the wedding hall was filled with guests.
>
> But when the king came in to see his guests, he noticed a man there who was not wearing wedding clothes.
>
> 'Friend,' he asked, 'how did you get in here without wedding clothes?' The man was speechless.
>
> Then the king told the attendants, 'Tie him hand and foot, and throw him outside, into the darkness, where there will be weeping and gnashing of teeth.'
>
> "For many are invited, but few are chosen."
> - Matthew 22:1-14

How many times have we refused the invitation of God on the basis of our pride? When we do come we clothe ourselves in *self*-righteousness rather than accepting his righteousness. In Jesus' day, guests of the wedding banquet were given clothes to wear to the banquet. To wear your own clothes would be an offense to your host, like saying, "Your clothes aren't good enough, I'll wear my own thanks." When we miss the mark, we are telling God that our values, plans, and priorities are more important – that we know better than he. That is not faith. That is arrogance.

Each one of us is inclined to preside as the ultimate authority of our own lives, and then we wonder why there is conflict in the world. We are most concerned with the best interest of self and we exercise our authority to provide it. Yet everyone else is doing the very same thing and so we contend with one another for what we presume we deserve.

As part of the strategy for getting what we need, want, and feel we are entitled to, we both give and take based on a value system we develop through our experiences. We identify needs and wants – though sometimes these lines are blurred (as in "I need a new car" vs. "I need food and water") – and we ascribe values to those things that determine how much we are willing to give in order to get what we want.

It comes down to the dynamic of economy. An economy is an exchange, a flow of give and take. It is what we are willing to give in order to obtain what we value. Every economy has a currency, or something that drives it. In our capitalist economy we give our currency of money in exchange for goods and services. We will shop for the best price on what we want because we do not want to pay more for something than we feel it is worth. We do the same on an emotional and spiritual level.

You don't have to be an economist to realize the trends of an economy. You live in it. You are steeped in it. We merely need to become intentional in how we function within a given economy. Nothing we know is an accident. Sure, there are scientists who will try to tell you that all we know is the result of a random process of evolution, but there are mathematicians who tell us that macro-evolution (the big bang, people descending from apes who are descended from pond scum) is a mathematical impossibility. Everything from grass, to trees, to bugs, birds, and people have purpose; there is intent.

Likewise, we need to be intentional in how we live and function in this highly structured world. The relationships among the human species are vastly different and more intricate than with any other species. Human relationships are special and need to be handled with purpose and care.

We need to realize that we are functioning, not just in a capitalist economy, but many different economies. Every economy in which we function, however, is driven by one. I've come to call this the economy of the soul. The economy of our soul is naturally focused on self. I use *my* wants, *my* hopes, *my* priorities, *my* desires, and *my* values to manage this economy…and so does everyone else.

The word of God through the prophet Isaiah hit it right on the head, "each has turned his own way." We have decided what is best and pursued it. It's the Garden of Eden personally replayed in each life. There are two ways to do anything, God's way and my way. The problem is that we have chosen "my way." In the Garden it was one little rebellious act enshrined forever in scripture as the severing of man's intimate relationship with God. Today, it is one everyday decision after another that merely perpetuates that separation.

This is not what God intended. He created the perfect environment to sustain us, and then created mankind in his image. Not that God looks like us, physically. Jesus took on *our* flesh; he bore *our* physical image and limitations. God is spirit and so it is his character and his attributes that his creation bears. This gift to us is meant to enable us to relate to God, to connect with him. We were created to know God, intimately, personally, and corporately. The beauty of it is that God does not *need* us. We are told in scripture of the love shared between the Father, the Son, and the Holy Spirit. The very essence of God's nature is love, and love is objective. Each member of what we call the Trinity holds the others as the object of perfect love and so God is complete and whole in and of himself. Those who teach that the Son and the Spirit are not God violate this essential truth and make God less than He is. God then becomes incomplete and we are reduced to a need. He created you because he *wants* you. You are desired.

—

Relationship is paramount to God. It is the foundation of his character, and it is the reason we exist. God is, himself, a relationship between the Father, the Son, and the Holy Spirit. The very essence of the Gospel of Christ is about a broken relationship between God and his creation and the lengths God has gone to restore that relationship. Once redeemed, we are commanded to grow in our relationship with God and foster healthy relationships with one another in order that the Gospel of Christ will spread and more people will be brought back into a right relationship with God.

Your basic purpose, therefore, is to know God through your growing, intimate relationship with him, and to make God known through your relationships with others as you reflect what you know of God in the way you live. An economy of self is a departure from this intent. Rather than putting God first and others second, we put self first, others last, and God is squeezed in where we deem convenient to us – if at all. We have reduced God to being a part of our life and we wonder why life seems so hard sometimes. We try to confine God to small corners of our lives and wonder why he doesn't show up where we need him most. The reason for all the suffering and strife in our world is the fact that we have missed the mark.

—

The reality is that we are a fallen, broken world desperately seeking to put the pieces back together. The greatest challenge we face is our own limitations. We clothe ourselves in our own values, our own priorities and moral code, and our own desires and expect God to accept them as his own. We acknowledge that others have a right to believe differently than we do, but we understand it's "to their detriment." This thinking has given birth to a new antichrist: Tolerance.

Tolerance sounds like a great idea. On the surface it seems to ask, "Can't we all just get along?" In reality, however, it looks very different. What tolerance actually says is, "You have your way, and I have mine. My way is better than yours or it wouldn't be my way. So you can be wrong or settle for less if you want to, and I'll just put up with you." As long as there is tolerance, we cannot have unity.

Unity comes only when we both choose the same way. But whose way do we use? By nature I feel my way is best, so I'm certainly not going to lay aside my way to go your stupid way. Yet you are thinking the very same thing. Our enemy, the devil, loves tolerance and will continue to feed it because tolerance prevents unity. In the world's economy of self, there can only be tolerance because no one will maintain the same value structure you do. Sure, you can find someone else who thinks that family is the highest priority, but they mean *their* family, not yours.

The persons of the Trinity have perfect unity. Therefore, as image bearers of God, we too are created for unity. The Bible refers to the church as a body, made up of many distinct and unique parts, but all forming one body. You are created and intended to be a part of a whole. We think that to be successful we must be the head, but that is not a good picture of success if you were created to be a foot. Feet don't make good heads. Nor does a spleen make a good lung. Could you imagine the breath you'd have? Success is when we realize our role and fulfill it regardless of what that is. Success for a screwdriver is tightening and loosening screws, not opening paint cans. Opening paint cans is more like a moral victory for a screwdriver; "Well, at least I did *something*."

—

A good picture of our world today would be a marathon. As all the runners move up to the starting line, the street is filled with bodies. Each one has a number and is wearing a uniform or costume that identifies them as an individual. Some uniforms look similar to others, but all are somehow unique. They move into position eager to begin the race and run for the prize. As the starting gun sounds they immediately take off, some bolt straight ahead, others turn left, some right, some run backwards, and some are just running in circles. As they each run their own way they are bumping and crashing into each other. Some are falling, others look more like a fullback crashing through the field of play, yet none of them are moving toward the finish line because they all have their own goal in mind – completely ignoring the course laid out for them.

This, of course, seems ridiculous. It's like something from a Monty Python movie, but it is what we do every day. We make our own rules, set our own course, and run our own race. Essentially, what makes organized sports so fun is the rules. There are rules that govern how the game is played so that everyone knows what is expected and how to win. Even the field of play has boundaries in order to allow the freedom to play hard and have success. We simply don't value the rules that we don't like or understand, and so we throw them out or rationalize why they do not apply to us.

Part of our problem is that we do not value that which we do not understand. For example, I never understood why some parents were so zealous to teach their children first-time obedience until someone's kid got hit by a car because they did not stop immediately when mom said to. Not understanding a thing makes it no less valid. We cannot see, touch, feel, hear, or taste gravity, but it is there and it applies whether we want to believe it or not. We can observe the effects of gravity, we can work with gravity to make planes fly, and we can experience the effects of gravity the same as we can the works and effect of God. And just like the presence and effect of God, we cannot live outside of the reality of gravity. Neither can you live outside the reality that life is not all about you.

—

Like the law of gravity, there are other laws that cannot be broken, other realities that we cannot escape no matter how fervently we deny them. Among these realities is that of community. You are not the center of the universe; nothing revolves around you. You are a part of a much bigger picture, and you need to know your place.

I despise waking up to find ants in my kitchen. When this occurs I initiate operations that wipe out countless thousands of these faceless creatures. Never once do I consider, even for a nanosecond, the history, accomplishments, purpose, or desires of a single one of these minions of thievery. What makes me think, that among so many people throughout mankind's history, I am any more significant than one of those ants? What makes an ant significant is not he himself. What makes the ant such a formidable opponent is not the greatness of any one. No, it is his place in the colony. He is a part of the whole and so they accomplish much.

We are a broken and fractured people, thinking only of our selves. We coexist, but we do not do so well. We have missed the mark of God's intent. It is easy enough to deem one's self a "good person" as we measure ourselves against those around us. We compile a list of evils we do not commit, however, it is not a human standard by which we are measured. The Bible says that, "all have sinned and fall short of the glory *of God*" (Romans 3:23, emphasis mine). It is God's standard by which we are measured. It is his image we are to reflect. We are to look like and live like God, not other fallen people.

The psalmist wrote, "The earth is the LORD's and everything in it; the world and all who dwell in it. For he founded it upon the seas, and established it upon the waters" (Psalm 24:1). All that is belongs to God. He made it, all of it; even you. He is the lawgiver and judge. He has shown us how this life is to be lived and what he has made us for and like that crazy marathon we have taken his gifts and run our own way with them. We have missed the mark of God's intent because we are aiming at the wrong target. Self is at the center of the economy of your soul, and I'm sorry, but you are too small a thing for life to be all about, even just *your* life. You are made for bigger things, to be part of a whole.

—

Before we can even touch on how we make the change, we need to understand the consequences of our economy of self. Consequences are a foreign concept to most people. We know what they are, but we fail to make the connection between our actions and future consequences. This is due in large part to our pride, our need to feel good about ourselves. We will deny the wickedness of our own actions in order to make ourselves appear "good enough." Have you ever been praying to God and glossed over the confession part of prayer? Have you ever said something like, "God, forgive me of my sin…" hoping the vagueness will hide the reality of guilt, or "forgive my wandering eyes," instead of naming your sins for what they are, like lust for example. We want to *be* acceptable to God. We do not want to have to be *made* acceptable by his grace.

There are severe consequences to this kind of self-centered thinking. We need to be confronted by those consequences and explore the dysfunction of the world's economy of self before we will realize the necessity for change. Change only becomes a desirable option when the status quo becomes too expensive to maintain or our guilt too great to bear.

Where have you missed the mark? Your whole life may be lived for yourself, in which case every area of your life is off target. Perhaps you have invited Christ into your life, but you have not surrendered your life to him and there are areas of your life in which you are maintaining control. We cannot cling to control in parts of our life and expect to experience peace and prosperity. We cannot try to control or contain God in little parts of our life and expect him to bless us as if we are faithful to him. We cannot edit God, taking only the parts of him we like, and presume to experience the power of his presence in our lives. We cannot know God if we aren't looking for him…if we are aiming at the wrong target.

We all need a wake-up call from time to time as God prepares to draw us closer and make us deeper. God accepts you just as you are, but he loves you far too much to just leave you like that. Unsettled feelings, shades of guilt, and an overwhelming sense of insufficiency are all just growing pains as God prepares to move you along in the process of coming alive. Conviction is an expression of pure love. And God so loves…you.

The Dysfunction of the Economy

—

"Youths oppress my people, women rule over them. O my people, your guides lead you astray; they turn you from the path. The LORD takes his place in court; he rises to judge the people."
~ Isaiah 3:12, 13

In case you had not noticed, our economy is in the toilet. As I write this in the middle of the year 2009, the jobless rate is as high as it's been since the 1940's, consumer confidence is down, housing prices are down, and it seems like no matter how low the Fed sets the interest rate, money is not moving. A thriving economy involves risk, and currently, no one is willing to take any. We are clinging to our money tightly because our future is so uncertain.

The world, indeed, is broken. Hunger and homelessness are prolific. Poverty and disease are rampant. Even in the heart of average suburban America there are many who are struggling with depression and loneliness. There are single parents who need community and youths who need guidance, and all of them are left to put the pieces of their broken lives together without guidance or direction. Sure, there are many social services around to fill the void, but in many cases, these people are just cases; they are a number, a statistic, or even a trophy.

In our church we have a good-sized group of "special education" members. These are people with Autism, Down's syndrome, and other handicaps that inhibit their learning ability and social integration. We affectionately call them "the boys," first, because they happen to be all guys; second because they are so child-like. It is delightfully refreshing to meet someone who is not hung up in the game of social acceptance. They simply are who they are, unashamed and without excuse or apology. I wish I were more like that.

It is amusing to watch the dynamic between them and people who aren't used to interacting with people like "the boys." Many people want to keep their distance, brush them off, or just avoid them as if what they have is contagious. The reality is most of these people feel it would cost too much to engage them. It is an investment they are not willing to make, so they check out.

We can appear a very compassionate culture. The reality is, however, that we can do some very good and charitable things for very selfish reasons. We'll give money to the guy on the corner because it is "right" or "good," but mostly because it's easy. Are we really doing that guy any good? How can we know if we don't take time to get to know him and his circumstance? But that would cost too much. It's much easier to smile, hand over a bill, and have your guilty conscience relieved than it is to actually care for and invest in someone else.

As I said before, we never like to pay too much for anything. When we see something we like in a department store we will go to Target or Wal-Mart to see if we can find it cheaper. Then we log on and scan Craigslist and eBay to see if we can get it cheaper still. In the same way, when we are presented with opportunities to invest ourselves in someone or something, we simply do not want to overpay. "Maybe" and "perhaps" are some of our favorite words because we can sound concerned or committed without actually committing to anything. We leave ourselves an out, a buffer, a safety net so we can safely check out when the cost gets too high.

There are other, more common arenas where people check out because they feel it costs more than they want to, or feel they should have to, pay. Living in an economy of self never affects only you. When a young couple finds out that nurturing a healthy marriage takes a lot of work and sacrifice, one takes off and the other is left with deep hurts and a skewed view of what love is supposed to be. When we discover that sex can be more than fun and an unexpected, unplanned child enters the picture we can check out and leave that child neglected, abused, or abandoned.

These examples may be extreme, but they are real. In the passage above, when Isaiah says, "Youths oppress my people and women rule over them," it is not a word against women or youth. It is a reality that when those who were supposed to invest themselves in the whole fail to do so and only seek out what they feel they are entitled to, those around them are left to fend for themselves. In doing so, they too, step outside God's order and intent and society suffers.

—

Sin is more than doing things you shouldn't. In fact, God's judgment in the Isaiah passage deals more with what Israel's leaders *aren't* doing. As it is written, "Anyone, then, who knows the good he ought to do, and does not do it, sins" (James 4:17). James is talking about a sin of omission. There are things that God requires of some, but not others. For me, I remember when God called me to abstain from alcohol of any kind. Now, the Bible never says, "Do not drink," it says, "Do not be drunk." Yet, God impressed this instruction on my heart and so for me, to drink is sin. There are both responsibilities and boundaries that God has placed in your life. They are for you as God works in your life personally, and to neglect those expectations or overstep those boundaries, for you, is sin and has measurable consequences, not only for you, but for those around you.

Gang activity is an increasing problem in our community. We aren't looking like LA yet, but it is getting worse. Gangs are formed for protection and profit. Young men are growing aware of power and influence, yet there is no one there to guide them and teach them how and when to use it. Dad is either not there at all, or, worse still, he is physically present but otherwise checked out — not doing "the good he ought to do." This missing influence begins a chain reaction that serves as a curse for the coming generations who will learn from their absentee fathers.

It's the same with young girls. Teen pregnancy is a very real problem. Because mom isn't there, or knows no better herself, or just doesn't care, these girls are left to figure life out on their own. This results in drop-outs, abortion, and abandonment. If these girls cannot finish school, they can't get jobs. If they cannot get jobs, they wind up on welfare, in and out of very unhealthy relationships, or living on the street making money the only ways they can: selling drugs or prostitution.

The increase of sexual immorality of many varieties is becoming overwhelming. We are sexual beings, but in the world's self-centered economy we shy away from healthy sex in a committed marriage relationship; that costs us too much and takes away our out. In our infinite wisdom we decide to serve our selves and meet our perceived needs by taking what we want and giving as little as we can. What happens is that God's gift of love is grossly miscommunicated through either neglect or abuse and the result is the wounded running to whatever will mask the pain, whether that is promiscuity or homosexuality or some other refuge like drugs or alcohol.

God is a God of order. When he had created everything he looked and saw that it was "very good." So what happened? As it is written in the prophet Isaiah, "We all, like sheep, have gone astray, each of us has turned to his own way" (Isaiah 53:6). If we are made to be one whole made up of many parts, yet we all go our own way, we are bound to be torn apart. We want to blame God for all the problems in the world. "If God was a God of love, then why are so many people starving and homeless?" "If God really cares, or is even there, why would he allow the terror attacks of September 11, 2001?" We give God all the blame for what is wrong, but take all the credit for the good ourselves. This way we can feel good about self and have a scapegoat for all our problems. The reality is, however, that it is God alone who has the right to ask us, "Why are so many of my people starving and homeless when you have so much yourself?" "Why do you kill each other when I have commanded you to love your neighbor *and* your enemy?"

The answer to these questions is that we think far too highly of ourselves. We value self over anyone else, so everyone else suffers for our lack of investment. Just as when consumer confidence is down and money isn't flowing the economy suffers, when we cling to our resources — our time, talent, and treasure — the spiritual economy of our world suffers as the poor, needy, and broken go bankrupt for want of simple, selfless kindness.

As I reflect on my own life, and I'm sure you can do this too, I find lingering under the rug and behind the dressers of my heart various regrets. Some of these are missed opportunities for glory. Let's be honest, we all have those "would-have, could-have, should-have" moments where we know we could have done better and perhaps become more if we only knew at that time what we know now. Yet the ones that I find the most painful at this point in my journey are the opportunities I have missed to really invest myself, to witness the power of God in and through me, and make a difference for the Kingdom of God — an eternal difference of eternal value. As a husband, a father, and a pastor, how many times have I chosen the safe route, the one that won't ask too much of me, the path of least investment? How many times have others continued to struggle for want of what I could have offered them?

In the gospels, we are told that Jesus feeds 5,000 men (not including the women and children) with five loaves and two fish. The point of that account is not that Jesus can feed your belly. It is less about God giving to you and more about you giving to God. Our self-centered economy wants to see that God will fill our stomachs and meet our needs, even when we can't see the resources to do so. What is remarkable about the account is the disciples' investment. They had enough food to take care of themselves. In Matthew, Mark, and Luke it looks like the disciples had the food with them. In John, it is a young boy who brings forward his lunch. In either case someone who had a little had to give it all over to Jesus. Our nature is to cling to our loaves and guard our fish. Once Jesus blessed the food, he gave it to the disciples to distribute. Again, they had the choice to pass it out to the masses, or keep it for themselves. It was not until the baskets left their hands and started making the rounds that they began to see the miracle. Had they clung to what was in their possession, thousands would have gone hungry. Yet as they let go and gave, they saw something only God could do, and they themselves, wound up with plenty.

As an example of one who got it wrong, Jesus told a parable of three servants in Matthew 25:14-30. Each was given an amount of resources to manage. Two seemed to do fine with it. The third, out of fear, buried his in the ground and wasted the opportunity to prove faithful. Jesus tells us that this servant was labeled as "wicked and lazy." Though it seems harsh, it makes clear God's view of taking his gifts to us and going our own way with them, using them, not for his glory, but our own. This is nothing shy of rebellion. It is a violation of God's order and, as we have covered, results in grievous consequences, not just for us, but for everyone around us — even generations to follow.

There are two ways we can live our lives: as a leaf, or a grape. Living for yourself in the world economy, looking after your own interests, desires, and comforts, is the way of the leaf. It is there for a while, but eventually falls to the ground and turns to dust. The leaf is mere existence. It bears no fruit. It delights in its beautiful fall colors ignorant that those colors are indicative of its death. When that time comes, it falls to the ground and is forgotten. It has amounted to nothing.

As I have said before, we know, inherently, that our lives are meant for more than that. We are meant to be grapes. The grape, too, may fall to the ground, but within the grape are several seeds. These seeds draw shelter and nourishment from the grape and each has the potential to sprout a vine which in turn produces many bunches of grapes. The grape is fruitful, productive, and useful as it makes a lasting impact and contributes to a lasting cycle of life.

We have strayed from our intended purpose and stepped outside God's order. In doing so, we have violated the integrity of society by tearing the fabric of community and fellowship; the very fabric of our existence. We are missing the mark of God's standard. We are missing out on his best and settling for a counterfeit because we are comfortable with it, never realizing that this comfort is indicative of our demise.

Getting back on target requires adjusting our aim. We must redirect the focus of the economy of our soul. It means that we need to become intentional about our decisions and motives. We need to connect and start living not in the smallness of our individual lives, but as a small, yet important and unique part of a whole. We need to start asking the right questions. Our inclination is to ask why we should not be able to do a thing or live a certain way. We need to start asking why we *should*.

In order to explore this new focus for our soul's economy we must first understand what drives the economy of our soul. This will require an open and honest searching of our deep heart. We avoid this at all costs because we are afraid of what we will find there. Often times we know we will not like what we find there and would rather sweep it under the rug and act like we do not see the unsightly bulge. Again, the economy of self wants desperately to be okay, to be right. We will make all manner of excuses, justifications, and compromises to maintain the appearance of rightness. The truth is… we can't afford to do that.

Chapter 2

The Currency of the Economy

A Currency of Fear

—

*"Therefore I tell you, do not worry about your life, what you
will eat or drink; or about your body, what you will wear.
Is not life more important than food, and the body more
important than clothes?"*
~ Matthew 6:25

What is it that drives the world's economy of self? Currency is
what drives any economy. The currency of our "goods and services"
capitalist economy is money. Everyone wants money, and no one
wants to lose it. We will do nearly anything for money. If you don't
believe me, just look at the myriad of "reality" shows on TV. Each
season, thousands of people are willing to endure extreme conditions
or extreme ridicule and humility for the chance to win money.
Storied sports franchises will change the name of their stadiums
to a sponsor's name for money. Disney will make any number of
embarrassingly bad sequels to movies that were supposed to have
ended "happily ever after" because there is profit to be had. We are
a society of sell-outs. Yet even the desire for money, as a part of the
world's economy of self, is driven by a deeper currency.

I was engaged twice in my life. The first time was during a period
where I was clearly invested in the world economy, as was the young

lady to whom I was engaged. My god was relationships. Hers was a good time. It is very hard to walk together on vastly different roads and over time, as we went our own ways, our relationship was torn apart. I cannot remember a more painful, unstable, fearful time in my life. I could see the writing on the wall, but was unwilling to admit my failure. I was afraid to fail and of what that would mean. I pretended it was working, but to no avail. I was afraid to lose her, afraid to live without her. I was afraid to keep her because the cost of maintaining the very fragile, dying relationship was way too high for me to keep up. I was a good person with good intentions but was completely consumed by the bad investments I had made.

There are a lot of good people enslaved by the world's economy. They have built their lives on the proverbial sand. As that foundation shifts and ebbs and moves, they become more and more fearful and work harder and harder to shore up their lives, but to no avail. It may look all good on the outside, but appearances are deceiving. We know that eventually all we have will fade away. The new car becomes old and we "need" to get a new one. The fine clothes become "this old thing" and it's time to shop. "Look and feel younger" immediately gets our attention because we are woefully aware of our own fading. We fear what we cannot control and we are surrounded by reminders that we can control far less than we would like to believe.

We have bought into a system that is broken. In the spiritual economy of our culture the currency is not as shallow as mere money. The currency is fear. Fear is what drives us. We are naturally fearful because we naturally see ourselves as far more important than we really are. We make too much of ourselves and too little of what really matters. Pride comes in two colors, "I'm so great," and "I'm so worthless." In either case, it is all about "me." We are raised in this mindset that the world revolves around "me." Me-first is at the heart of every sin whether it is a sin of commission (something you do) or a sin of omission (something you neglect to do). We step into these sins based on one simple criterion: "What's in it for me?"

—

Nowhere is the currency of fear more obvious than in the gang culture. It is fear that drives these young people to come together.

They want the protection of a family, but they don't feel they are getting that at home, so they seek safety in numbers outside a healthy home context. They fear that they will not achieve significance or financial stability, so they come together to secure it by whatever means they can. Fear drives their actions and dictates their endeavors. Conversely, they rely on the fear of others to get what they want.

On a less obvious scale, each one of us does the very same thing. Our need for acceptance and significance drives us to measure ourselves by the standard of the world: what we should look like, how we should dress, the car we should be driving, the job we should have, and the people we should associate with. These things cease to be a *part* of our lives — resources within our lives — and they become the standard by which we measure our worth and find our identity. Fear compels us to pursue various things we determine to be valuable, and if we put up a good enough front we can use the fear of others to glean what we need from them.

I've seen this dynamic at work even within the church. Someone comes in seeking, not Jesus, but acceptance, authority, and significance. They bring in a worldly standard of success and begin to "climb the ladder." Once they come to a place where they are challenged, convicted, and being held accountable, they determine that the cost is too high and they move on to less authentic pastures where they can join the club and play the game and achieve an empty measure of success.

Not everyone guilty of this trend does so maliciously; in fact, usually not. Based on temporal possessions and ever-changing trends we form an image of self that we believe will make us both important and happy. We ascribe far too much value to material possessions and the opinions of others and we take upon ourselves a burden we were never meant to carry, one that will drain us of all our time and energy and life. We invest so much in this false self that we are afraid to let it down; we are fearful that someone might discover who we really are, that we will not have the strength to keep up the act. Fear becomes our motivation; it becomes the measure for what we will or will not invest in. It determines when it is time to cut our losses and move on to a "safer" environment.

"Do not store up for yourselves treasures on earth, where moth and rust destroy, and where thieves break in and steal. But store up for yourselves treasures in heaven, where moth and rust do not destroy, and where thieves do not break in and steal. For where your treasure is, there your heart will be also.

The eye is the lamp of the body. If your eyes are good, your whole body will be full of light. But if your eyes are bad, your whole body will be full of darkness. If then the light within you is darkness, how great is that darkness!"

~ Matthew 6:19-23

Fear and idolatry go hand in hand. When we violate God's order and make anything other than him the main thing, we step outside the harbor of his protection and faithfulness. He remains, like the father of the prodigal son, poised to embrace us when we return to him, but he lets us bear the burden of our choices as well. When the world becomes not just a good thing, but the ultimate thing, life becomes much less stable. There is freedom in surrender. There is something to be gained in letting go.

—

Fear drives our decisions because we have undergirded our lives with dying things. Our lives are so fragile because the materials we are building with do not last, but we boast that they will. It seems that we are okay with this façade as long as we can appear that we are successful and in control. The problem with living in a fear-driven economy is that our priorities shift as we encounter things that we are more afraid of.

In JRR Tolkien's *The Lord of the Rings*, there is a character named Grima Wormtongue. He has aligned himself with the wizard Saruman who has betrayed Middle-Earth to serve the Dark Lord Sauron. Grima's subjection to Saruman is based on fear. The wizard orders this man around like a dog who obeys with his tail between his legs. It is not until the fear of defeat and insignificance overwhelms Grima that he turns on and attacks Saruman. Though Grima's loyalties shifted, the driving motive behind his decisions did not. He was not driven by justice, chivalry, or honor. He was still driven by fear. Likewise, our lives are governed by our fears. The things we are afraid of are ever-changing as we gain new experiences or add more to our lives, but make no mistake, I choose to do, and not do, based on fear. And so do you.

God does not want us to be driven by our fears. Three hundred and sixty-five times in scripture we are admonished not to fear. Fear takes our focus off of God and puts it on the things of the world as they pertain to us. Through this lens, things like truth are continually knocked out of focus. Our hearts grasp for anything that might provide some stability and more often than not, we wind up making really bad investments.

There is a wonderful account in scripture that illustrates this point. Jesus gets in a boat with his disciples to cross the sea of Galilee and continue preaching and teaching to towns on the other side. We will pick up when an unexpected and unwelcome event intrudes:

> "A furious squall came up, and the waves broke over the boat, so that it was nearly swamped. Jesus was in the stern, sleeping on a cushion. The disciples woke him and said to him, 'Teacher, don't you care if we drown?'
>
> He got up, rebuked the wind and said to the waves, 'Quiet! Be still!' Then the wind died down and it was completely calm.
>
> He said to his disciples, 'Why are you still so afraid? Do you still have no faith?'
>
> They were terrified and asked each other, 'Who is this? Even the wind and waves obey him?'"
>
> ~ Mark 4:34-41

There is a great temptation to make the accounts of scripture an allegory for our lives. We adopt a "me-ology" and insert ourselves, or apply the illustration to our lives assuming we understand what is being said. We assume that the boat is our life, the storm is our difficult circumstance or trying season and that Jesus calms the storms of our lives. Though there is a degree of truth to that thinking, we must not cheapen scripture by reducing it to a favorable allegory.

The storm that came upon the disciples was life-threatening. Think, "Hurricane Katrina." This is not your difficult season of life, a trying circumstance, or a rocky relationship. These seasoned fishermen, who were raised on the Sea of Galilee, were convinced that they were going to die. This is the raw and uncontrollable power of nature unleashed.

The point of this account is that Jesus came for a reason; the twelve were chosen for a purpose. All this was ordained by God, the only One greater than this storm. The test was to see if the disciples would trust Jesus and the power and plan of God or if they would look within to their own ability, skill, and understanding. They failed. What drove their decision to cry out to Jesus was the fear that all they had invested was insufficient and they were about to be exposed. Everyone who said they were crazy for following this upstart Rabbi would be validated. They would be remembered as simple fishermen who became statistics instead of anything special as they had hoped. They failed to trust Jesus and despaired.

In Jesus' rebuke of the storm, he demonstrated that God is greater than the greatest thing they knew, and they need not fear. Just trust and obey. It is a lesson I am learning myself. God is greater than the greatest things I know, more powerful than all I can experience or comprehend. Nothing can frustrate God's plan and purpose and the challenge is to live like I believe that.

Our fears oppose our faith. They lead us away from God. Greater than the power of the storm, which can topple structures, rend a boat, and kill the body, was the power of fear and doubt in the disciples' hearts. Jesus first rebuked the storm, and then their fear.

Upon seeing the power of God in Jesus, they asked, "Who is this?" Fear is born of ignorance.

—

With so many things in this world vying for our attention and devotion, it is easy for God to become lost to us...or more accurately, for us to become lost to God. We may know God exists — we have a belief — but we do not *know* him. Because we do not know him, we cannot really love or trust him and so our focus and attention is drawn to other things made readily available to us; things we can see, hear, touch, taste, and smell. We come to think so highly of ourselves and so much of the things that have come to define our lives that we lose sight of God. No wonder the wind and waves is all we can see at times. The only solid, stable, unshifting thing we can find can't be found by our distracted soul. Our hearts are drowning in an ocean of things that will drain our physical, emotional, and spiritual bank accounts and leave us empty and unfulfilled.

"Above all else, guard your heart, for it is the wellspring of life" (Proverbs 4:23). There is nothing more precious than our heart. In biblical language, the heart is so much more than the muscle that pumps blood through your body. It is the very seat of your mind, strength, and emotion —the essence of who you are. It is precious to God, who treasures who you are over anything you can do. Yet out of our fears — fear of failure, fear of success, fear of rejection, fear of exposure, fear of not getting our due —we grant heart access to so many people and things that simply are not worthy of it. In our fear we seek to protect ourselves and preserve a level of safety and comfort never realizing that we are actually betraying our heart into the hands of murderers. Everything we thought would bring us joy and freedom has actually enslaved us and is killing our deep heart. That is what Jesus meant when he said, "If then the light within you is darkness, how great is that darkness!" He is talking about the death of your heart by sacrificing it to unworthy things.

If your heart is given over to fear, it cannot be given to God. There is a decision to be made. "Will I continue to buy into the world's economy and live my life according to what it says I need and who it says I am supposed to be, or will I surrender my life to God, who created me, and knows exactly who I am supposed to be?" The opposite of fear is faith, and faith is an intentional decision to believe that God is who he says he is and to trust that he is faithful to do all he has promised. To choose faith is seldom easy...otherwise there would really be no need for faith. But it is always worth it.

Trusting God demands risk. As the disciples feared and woke the Lord that fateful night on the Sea of Galilee, their question was one of desperation. English translations render their question along the lines of, "Don't you care that we are drowning?" In Greek, there are three ways to phrase a question. One simply asks the question with no indication of the expected response. The other two imply that a certain response is expected. A question beginning with μη (may) implies the speaker expects a "no." If the question begins with ου (ou), as with the disciples in this account, the speaker expects a positive response. Their question is better translated, "You *do* care if we drown, *don't you?*"

We tend to relate to God this same way. We want to believe that he has our best interest in mind, but we are afraid he does not because what he knows is best seldom looks like what we think is best. We ask him, "Lord, you do care, don't you? You do want what is best for me, don't you? You do want for me what I want, right?" All the while, he is looking at us with love and compassion and in grace he asks us, "You do want what *I* want, don't you? You of little faith, why are you still so afraid?"

—

Fear drives us to guard the fragile and wounded parts of our life. We refuse to give God access because we do not trust him. The result is that God becomes merely a part of our life, if involved at all. We cannot connect with him, hear him, or see him at work because we are so focused on the things we want and the things we can control. We will never find freedom or accomplish anything significant or meaningful and lasting if we are clinging to things and keeping them from God — or God from them. To be Christian is to be surrendered to God, completely surrendered and willing to grant him access to every part of our life and heart.

Our lives have become a quest for meaning, purpose, and happiness. We cannot find these things if our focus remains on the things we can control and if our life is governed by the fear of the things we cannot. We need to place our trust in the One who is greater than the greatest thing we know. We need to trust him and actually live like we trust him to realize the abundant life we all somehow know we were intended to have.

There has been a lot so far that is difficult to hear and facilitates a great level of conviction. Hang in there. This was hard for me to hear and process too. In fact, I am still being challenged, convicted, changed, shaped, and molded. You do not have to be afraid to ask God, "You do care about these fragile parts of my heart, don't you?" When he answers you and says, "Why are you so afraid, you of little faith?" realize that this in an invitation. We have to realize and admit there is a problem, identify the symptoms of that problem, and then diagnose the problem itself before we can get treatment and find healing. The Bible calls this process confession, repentance, and restoration or renewal. To some, I want to assure you that you are not alone in this journey. To others, I want to assure you that you are not exempt from it.

A Word on Fear

—

"God did not give us a spirit of fear, but a spirit of power, of
love and of self discipline."
~ 2 Timothy 1:7

When dealing with certain terms, it is important to define what we are talking about. It is easy to presume we know what a word means and then press on in the wrong direction because our understanding varies from that of the presenting party.

Did you know there are two types of anger? Righteous anger is when you are upset on behalf of someone else for their good. Then there is selfish anger that is born of pride. There are also two types of pride. One is when you are pleased with someone or something and delight in them, as in, I am proud of my daughter because she plays piano so beautifully. The other kind of pride is when we think of ourselves more highly and/or more often than we ought to. There are two types of love. There is the emotional romantic love of the world which we fall in and out of, and there is true, biblical love which is an intentional attitude that considers what is best for the other person. In the case of our topic here, there are two types of fear. The first is an unhealthy fear, the kind that drives our economy of self. This fear is fed by one of two things: Guilt and shame, or ignorance.

—

When we look at the beginning of sin in the Garden of Eden, we see Adam and Eve, having eaten from the forbidden tree, trying to cover their shame and nakedness with self-made coverings of fig leaves. When they heard the sound of God walking in the garden, they hid.

When God calls out to them, not looking for their geography, but for them — their heart and the intimacy they had shared — their response reveals the heart of the matter.

"Then the man and his wife heard the sound of the
LORD God as he was walking in the garden in the

cool of the day, and they hid from the LORD God
among the trees of the garden. But the LORD God
called to the man, 'Where are you?'

He answered, 'I heard you in the garden, and I was
afraid because I was naked; so I hid.'"

~ Genesis 3:8-10

Adam knew he had blown it. Rather than deal with it, the fear
produced by his guilt led him to hide. It was not enough to weave
leafy briefs to cover his naked body; he also hid among the trees.
Later, he would throw his wife, Eve, under the bus and blame her for
what happened, no doubt damaging his relationship with her.

Fear is a self-made prison. We fail or rebel, and then we hide.
When you cannot trust the authority over you, you will lie and
deceive or hide in order to avoid trouble. I can remember many times
as a child I would blame "I don't know" for the broken trinkets and
missing tools. It got easier when I got a little sister. Then I could
just blame her. My parents always told me things would be easier
and simpler if I just told the truth, but fear wouldn't let me. I had
to hide my guilt.

We hide in part because we are afraid of disappointing others,
and in part to hide our weaknesses and failures. Remember, by
nature we are hopelessly self-centered. "Me-first." We want to believe
that we are good, in, or okay. Therefore, we will do what we need
to in order to keep up that façade, whether it is lying, or blaming
someone or something else.

In Hebrews, it is written that we are to "cast off everything
that hinders and the sin that so easily entangles and run with
perseverance the race marked out for us" (Hebrews 12:1). That idea
of entanglement needs to be clear to us. When we sin, we begin to
weave a web of deception to cover it up. What we are really doing,
however, is entangling ourselves in sin after sin. Rather than hiding
our guilt and finding freedom, we pile on the guilt and shame and
enslave ourselves to the very thing we want freedom from.

Adam sinned when he failed Eve at the tree. He sinned again
when he ate of the fruit. He sinned further when he made coverings

for them and then hid from God. He sinned yet again when he pointed the finger at Eve *and God*, "It was the woman *You* put here with me" (Genesis 3:12, emphasis mine). One sin on top of another, each one an effort to hide, just buried Adam deeper and deeper, wounding his heart over and over again, making him more and more afraid.

This is not a healthy fear of God. This is the kind of fear that calls God's heart into question. This is the kind of fear that paralyzes and enslaves. This is the kind of fear that drives you away from God and it is a weapon of the enemy. It may look like a good and logical idea at times, but remember, Satan too can masquerade as an angel of light. As it is written, "There is a way that seems right to a man, but in the end it leads to death" (Proverbs 14:12). This is definitely the way that leads to death. The greater our fear, the stronger the temptation to run from God, the One who can actually heal our heart, soul, mind, and strength. Apart from his mercy and grace, we will perish in our sin.

—

Unhealthy fear is also bred through ignorance. As we have seen with the disciples in the boat, when Jesus rebuked the storm, and then rebuked their fear, the question on their minds was, "What kind of man is this?" (Mark 4:41). Though they had experienced so much, they still had no idea who Jesus really was and what it all meant. They knew some things about Jesus, even knew him a little bit, but they were missing the big picture, and they failed to have faith. They could not trust Jesus with their lives at that point because they were ignorant — they did not understand who he was or why he was there.

In the disciples' panic during that storm, they displayed ignorance on a number of levels. To begin with, they were ignorant of God's sovereignty. It is one thing to acknowledge that God is in control when things are going well; it is quite another to affirm the same truth when the wheels come off. Remember, Jesus told the disciples to get into the boat. His instruction was to go to the other side. Do you think that Jesus had no idea what was going to happen? He was already foretelling his arrest, death, and resurrection. Did the storm catch him unaware? Not likely.

God *causes* trying circumstances. Does that bother you? God commanded Abram to offer his son, Isaac. God hardened, or strengthened, Pharaoh's heart against the children of Israel. God led Gideon to reduce 30,000 men to 300 men and then led them to fight countless thousands. The Father sent his one and only Son to die on the cross for sins he never committed. God is sovereign. Your trial, your circumstance, is an opportunity to test and teach you. You learn best through adversity; those lessons stick with you. Additionally, when God tests you, it is not for him to figure out what you're made of; it is for you to learn what you're made of. Trial can reveal many things: good, bad, and ugly. That test can affirm, encourage, or convict and lead you to repentance, as God did in 2 Chronicles 7:13-14.

> "When I shut up the heavens so that there is no rain, or command locusts to devour the land or send a plague among my people..."

Did you catch that? When who causes what? And what is the purpose?

> "if my people, who are called by my name, will humble themselves and pray and seek my face and turn from their wicked ways, then I will hear from heaven and will forgive their sin and will heal their land."

The purpose is to heal the people. God is far more concerned with your holiness than he is with your happiness. He wants to heal you — your heart — and will use whatever he needs to do so. This brings us to the second area of ignorance that feeds our unhealthy fear: we are ignorant of God's heart.

The disciples' question in the Greek is best rendered, "You do care that we are perishing don't you?!?" They wanted to know that Jesus cared about them and their condition. It is the human condition. We all, regardless of cultural or chronological context, want to know that we matter, that we are cared about, loved. We want to believe that there would be people who would miss us if we were gone or missing. We deeply desire significance. How many times have you heard (or maybe asked) the question, "God, if you really care about me, then why...?" When things don't measure up to our expectation, when things go wrong, it is hard to see God's care and compassion, but very easy to assume he doesn't care. We doubt his heart for us.

The Bible consistently teaches that God uses all things — good, bad, and ugly — for our good. It is a concept that we can grasp and agree with...until such a time that we really need to. When times are hard, Romans 8:28 can sound trite, but it's not. God certainly can, and does, use all things for the good of those whose hearts are devoted to him. The goal in all this, as pointed out earlier, is not your happiness, your worldly prosperity, your comfort, or even your physical health. The goal is your heart. "For those God foreknew he predestined to be conformed into the likeness of his Son" (Romans 8:29). Christ-likeness is the goal — an eternal goal. You are a small but important part of a whole and God has in mind, not just your good, but what is best for you and for the whole: what the Bible calls "the common good" (1 Corinthians 12:7). We can trust God's heart even when we don't understand it. Who wants a God they can fully understand? He'd be no more than we are.

Jesus answered the disciples' question with a question. "Why are you still afraid? Do you still have no faith?" (Mark 4:40) Our lack of belief and trust (faith) will fracture our relationship with God. The disciples asked Jesus, "You do care about us, don't you?" Jesus in turn asked the disciples, "You do trust me, don't you?" If we distrust God's heart, we will never realize the abundant life he has called us to because we will always be second-guessing God and trying to take matters into our own hands.

Trying to gain control of our circumstances ourselves alludes to the third area of ignorance that culminates fear in our lives: we are ignorant of God's ability. Ephesians 3:20-21 tells us that that God can do immeasurably more than anything we could ask for, or even possibly imagine. If you can think it up, God can do it. Whether he does or not goes back to the other two areas, his sovereignty and his heart to do what is best. The disciples in the boat knew Jesus as a teacher and a healer. They did not know him as the Creator and Sustainer of all creation. Do you? Do you understand that there is nothing that is impossible for God? I think we often know we are supposed to know and believe that, but do we live like we believe that? I know, it's hard. I struggle with this one still myself. I find myself putting my ignorance on display when I fear to act because I question God's sovereignty, heart, or ability in some way. However, I have also overcome that fear at times…and so can you.

At the last supper, the disciples still had very little idea of Jesus' mission. In ignorance, they made bold assertions that they would die with Jesus if necessary; but in the moment of truth, they failed, thought only of themselves, and fled, leaving Jesus alone. Their fear was born of ignorance. They were ignorant of Jesus' purpose, of his sovereignty — that he was laying down his life, not having it taken from him — and of their role in the kingdom. Later, as they were hiding in locked rooms or a rekindled fishing career, their fear was compounded by guilt and shame. This fear overwhelmed them and governed their decisions, and ultimately, their lives…until something extraordinary happened.

—

That Saturday had to have been the longest day of the disciples' lives. Jesus had been in the tomb only one night, but that was more than enough time to marinate and steep in their fear and failure. The Sabbath was meant to be a day of rest, but there was no rest in the hearts of the men who had called Jesus "teacher" and "friend." Their minds were laboring over all that went wrong (and that could go wrong in the near future) as the fear began to saturate their hearts and dim their view of God's light. Imagine their surprise Sunday morning when the women came back early from the tomb where they had gone to finish preparing Jesus' body for burial, breathless and in a terrified, but slightly excited fervor.

All the disciples, the men and the women alike, were confused and frightened by the events of the crucifixion. Yet that Sunday morning, Jesus began to heal their fear, and it began with Mary Magdalene. She came to the tomb to find the body of Jesus. Even when she saw that it was gone, she was desperate to find the body, to take charge of the body. What little hope she had left hung on finding Jesus' dead body. While she stood in the garden weeping — venting fear through tears — Jesus confronted her, "Woman, why are you crying?" Then, as she began to explain, it came. "Mary." He called her by name. At that moment, fear turned to joy. The confusion still there, the uncertainty still looming, but this personal encounter with the Lord Jesus had replaced fear with unspeakable joy. She *had* to tell the others.

When Mary arrived at the disciples' hiding place, she began to share her overwhelming joy. The guys, of course, did not believe her, until Jesus was suddenly standing among them. In spite of shut windows and locked doors, there he was. The disciples had no idea what was happening (though it had been told to them by Jesus several times before), nor did they understand what the babbling Mary had been raving about, but now Jesus was here, among them. They saw and believed. Thomas was not with them. He too doubted — just as the others had — and when he saw, he believed too. Likewise, there were those two on the road to Emmaus. They also encountered Jesus but at first did not recognize him. They told him, "We *had hoped* he was the one..." (Luke 24:21, emphasis mine). Jesus then began to unpack the scriptures for them, revealing the plan fulfilled in Jesus. When they finally recognized Jesus, they were elated. Their fear and doubt were replaced with the same joy that had filled Mary's heart.

What all these encounters have in common is the fact that Jesus confronted the ignorance of the disciples. His words to his followers upon this revelation was, "Stop doubting and believe!" There comes a time when God has given us all the evidence we need, all the facts required, and we simply need to get off the fence and make the choice to trust. Jesus encounters us personally, and then confronts our ignorance; then he confronts our guilt and shame.

No religious system deals with the burden of our guilt and shame. We cannot deny that burden is there, but we will often choose a religious system that puts relief in our own hands through good works or one that hides sin under the rug of spirituality, karma, and/or natural process. Only Jesus Christ deals with our guilt and shame.

Only he will give us the relief — the freedom — we desperately need and secretly long for.

Though many of the questions the disciples had were answered through their encounters with Jesus, there was a lingering guilt and shame that drove them to hide in their fishing careers. Now understanding who Jesus is, they felt of no use to him for their failure. Peter went back to fishing and led others to follow him. It was there that Jesus confronted their guilt and shame.

When Jesus met the disciples on the beach at the Sea of Galilee, they came in expecting to find judgment and reprimand; what they received was grace. It came in the form of a campfire, a hot meal, and a warm invitation from a good friend. Jesus even took Peter aside and very gently gave him an opportunity to declare his love for his Lord, once for each public denial. Each time, Jesus also gave Peter hope and purpose as he commissioned him to shepherd his flock, the church. Jesus never wants us to simply "let go" of our guilt and shame, to dismiss it as if it doesn't matter. He died for your guilt. He suffered and bore your shame. It matters. He does want us, though, to surrender it to him and bear it no more. To do that, we need to both know him and trust him. Your sin and failure are never beyond the healing grace of the Lord Jesus Christ.

Most of the time, we operate out of fear born of ignorance, or remain driven to cover our guilt and shame and we simply fail to identify it as such. These two realities serve as the source of our fears. Unless we correct them through a personal encounter with Jesus (a first time encounter or a deeper encounter) that confronts our ignorance and heals our guilt and shame, we will never find freedom, hope, or purpose and value in the kingdom of God. Not all fear, however, is bad. In fact, there is a case where fear can be the beginning of something beautiful.

Healthy Fear

—

The second type of fear is a healthy fear. It is the kind of fear we are commanded to have before God, the kind we cannot help but have when we truly encounter the living God. This begins, as it did with Isaiah, with a sense of being afraid — the other kind of fear. Isaiah, when he encountered God in the temple, said, "Woe to me! I am ruined! For I am a man of unclean lips, and I live among a people of unclean lips, and my eyes have seen the King, the LORD Almighty." (Isaiah 6:5)

Isaiah was confronted by his guilt and shame in light of the holiness and majesty of God. In that moment he was overcome with fear as he realized there was nowhere to hide and bore before God the weight of his guilt and the burden of the consequences of his sin. Isaiah assumed he would die before holy God for his sin, and if not for the grace of God, he would have.

That sense of fear, realizing that the author of life and the holy Judge of all creation sees through your leafy briefs to your guilt and shame, *should* be terrifying. We need to understand the consequences of our sin and rebellion. We need to be confronted with the reality of what we deserve in order to understand the depth and richness of the mercy and grace God has given us.

Healthy fear, like any healthy organism, grows and develops over time. What began for Isaiah — and many others like him — as a terrifying encounter with the reality of the holiness and presence of almighty God ended with adoration and reverent fear, secure in the knowledge of God's mercy and grace. Unhealthy fear, "afraid" fear, doesn't develop. It stunts our growth and tightens its strangle hold on our heart. Only when we lay it out before God, as Isaiah did, can God move us past that and into healthy, reverent fear. In Isaiah's encounter, God addressed Isaiah's ignorance of God's person, sovereignty, and ability and then addressed the issue of his guilt and shame. Isaiah was healed and ready for action.

Unhealthy fear is, essentially, worry gone wild. Worry, basically, is concern that has consumed us. God wants us to be concerned. When we pair concern with compassion, the love of Jesus is revealed.

All these emotions God has given us are to spur us "toward love and good deeds" (Hebrews 10:24). They are like the lights on your dash board. Recently, the "check engine" light came on in my car. It's an old 1997 Ford Escort station wagon with 135,000 miles and it has its issues. The light tells me that it is time to do something about at least one of those issues. The light on the dash is an indicator, not the engine. I cannot drive the car nor determine the car's fate by that one light. The light is just letting me know something needs to be looked at. Our emotions are the same thing, an indicator that something is going on beneath the surface, and we need to take a look.

God may have given me this car — this life — to drive, but he is the manufacturer, owner, and mechanic. When the lights start going on, I bring the car of my life in to him. I can maintain both my real car and the car of my life. I can top off the fluids, fill the gas tank, clean the windows and keep the kid's trash in the back seat at bay. But more is needed, so it goes to the One who can fix it.

When we openly and willingly bring our fear to God, he transforms that unhealthy fear into a healthy fear that will serve as a nutrient in the soil of our heart so that when we receive the seed of God's word, we will take it in and bear fruit. Healthy fear is required to bear lasting fruit — for seeing a good return on God's investment. If we do not fear God, then he remains that cute and loving grandfather figure in the clouds that we visit when it's convenient and call twice a year out of obligation. Healthy fear keeps God and us each in our proper place. He is Lord and Master, we are children and servants. We obey out of fear.

Healthy fear is not always fear of punishment or judgment. Country music often illustrates the other side of healthy fear (too often, since they describe carnal love instead of godly love). It is what I call the "I can't possibly go on without you" ideology. Fear of God is very often a fear of being separated from him. For those who have walked with God for any period of time, going back to life without him is terrifying. Sometimes I find myself afraid to make certain decisions because I don't want to make the wrong one and step outside of God's will and purpose. That can be good in that it indicates my desire is for God. It can be a problem because God is not afraid of my failures and I need to trust him to use my wrong decisions to draw me closer to him and teach me.

We need a healthy fear of God. We must see God for who he is and recognize his holy greatness, but also his holy goodness. We must acknowledge the reality of judgment, but also the reality of mercy and grace. We must honor and revere God, and at the same time trust him and love him. This takes time and experience…and more than one step of faith.

Using Foreign Currency

—

"The LORD *enters into judgment against the elders and leaders*
of his people: "It is you who have ruined my vineyard; the
plunder from the poor is in your houses. What do you mean
by crushing my people and grinding the faces of the poor?"
declares the Lord, the LORD *Almighty."*
~ Isaiah 3:14-15

During my time in the Marine Corps, I was stationed in Japan.
To make life easier and eliminate the need for math, I exchanged
my dollars for Yen. Yen is the Japanese currency and it is much easier
to get along when you make the exchange. When I returned to the
States, what Yen I had left made a great souvenir, but it was not legal
tender. To keep a few Yen in my pocket in case I needed it would be
foolish. Yet this is what many of us do in the spiritual economy.

The church is intended to be vastly distinct from the world
around it. We are to be *in* the world and among its citizens, but not
of the world or partakers of the world's economy. The Bible puts
it this way, "No longer be conformed to the pattern of this world,
but be transformed by the renewing of your mind" (Romans 12:2).
Unfortunately, the church — in so many cases — looks a lot like the
world. So many Christians are also undermined by fear.

Like our capitalist economy, the Christian life is a life of
uncertainty. God has warned us, "'For my thoughts are not your
thoughts, neither are your ways my ways,' declares the LORD. 'As
the heavens are higher than the earth, so are my ways higher than
your ways and my thoughts than your thoughts'" (Isaiah 55:8-9).
Because God just doesn't do things the way we would want or
expect, we never know what's coming.

Because of our natural sense of self-preservation, we, like the rest
of the world, will incline to cling to what we have. Like the wicked
and lazy servant in Matthew 25, out of fear we hide away that which
was entrusted to us and fail to do what would please the Master. We
put self before God or anyone else and seek to save our nice little
lives. We take in and take in through sermons, Bible studies, prayer

meetings, books, and small groups but never pour out — we attend church without stepping out to be the church. We become like a pond with only an inlet. The water comes in and sits. The lack of current allows bacteria and algae to grow and collect and we get a thick layer of pond scum. The last thing the world needs, and God wants, is scummy Christians.

Like our real world economy, when there is no flow of currency, the society as a whole suffers. The message is not spread, the hurting are not healed, the sinner does not repent, and the enemy's hold is not loosened. As it is written in Matthew 25:41-46,

> "Then he will say to those on his left, 'Depart from me, you who are cursed, into the eternal fire prepared for the devil and his angels. For I was hungry and you gave me nothing to eat, I was thirsty and you gave me nothing to drink, I was a stranger and you did not invite me in, I needed clothes and you did not clothe me, I was sick and in prison and you did not visit me…I tell you the truth, whatever you did not do for the least of these, you did not do for me.'"

The people's response to God's judgment was, "Lord, when did we see you…?" They call him Lord but don't even recognize him when he shows up in their lives! These people have assumed they are God's but are not. So many have made the assumption that they belong to God simply because they attend church and have done enough to feel comfortable and safe — good enough — but they do not demonstrate that they belong to God and follow Jesus.

When we fail to act on our faith, we contribute to the failure of our spiritual economy, to the detriment of the whole. With the gift of salvation comes a responsibility to act. When we read the Isaiah 3 passage for what it really says, we realize that God was not talking to the outside world. It should be no surprise that the enemies of God would violate His order and experience the consequences. You cannot expect pigs to bleat like sheep. But through the prophet

Isaiah, God was delivering a very hard word to His beloved people — to the church.

—

We have been raised in the world and the world's economy comes naturally to us. When we come to Jesus and trade in our currency of fear for the currency of the Kingdom, we often cling to some of our fear, just in case we might need it. That fear begins to compound and pretty soon we find it very difficult to pull currency out of our pocket and find Kingdom currency among all the fear.

As Jesus taught the crowds at the Sermon on the Mount, there was a mixed group. There were those who simply wanted what Jesus would give them, and those who genuinely wanted to draw nearer to God. Some wanted their nice little lives and to get out of hell and others were willing to forsake their lives to have God. There were those who "attended church," and those who longed to live out the truth and commands of God. As he taught, Jesus made a very profound statement. He said, "No one can serve two masters. Either he will hate one and love the other, or he will be devoted to one and despise the other. You cannot serve both God and Money" (Matthew 6:24).

The word we translate "money" is μαμωνα (*mamona*, or mammon). The word refers to money or wealth, but personified, like an idol. We understand that we are saved by grace alone through faith alone in Christ alone, that it is Jesus only and not "Jesus and…" Once we are saved into the Kingdom, however, we live "Jesus and…" We choose God because we know we should, but we serve self and guard our safety and comfort because we feel we need to. Our hearts are divided by the fear of judgment and punishment and our desires for our lives. We know we should want God, but we still cling to the things we can manipulate and control, like money or ministry or superficial relationships. In this divided allegiance, we live under the authority of "Jesus and…"

—

It is not easy to make the exchange from the world economy and its currency of fear to a Kingdom economy and its currency of faith. It comes naturally to us to assume that since we prayed a prayer and maintain some religious habits that we are no longer our "old self." The truth is, however, that our natural inclination can, and often does, deceive us.

> "Enter through the narrow gate. For wide is the gate and broad is the road that leads to destruction, and many enter through it. But small is the gate and narrow is the road that leads to life, and only a few find it."
>
> ~ Matthew 7:13-14

The wide gate, the broad road — these are easy. It comes so naturally to travel them. You don't have to look to find it. It is the path of least resistance. You need not "ask, seek, and knock" to get there. Just follow the crowd and settle for the socially acceptable "norm."

Parts of the broad road seem narrower than others, and it seems easy to wander from the narrow to the broad. Let the sincere become routine and the passionate pursuit become mundane habit and there you are.

When I first got involved in ministry, I was on fire to make God known. It didn't take long, however, for that zeal to conform to the world's standards and morph into a desire for ministry success, a need to be liked and accepted, a numbers game. When other pastors became my standard instead of Jesus, I began to realize that I had left the narrow road. When people would ask how my church was doing and I spoke of attendance numbers and budget figures, I started to see that my focus was all wrong. That's what everyone else was doing. In fact, that's how successful businesses do it in the world, and that was the problem.

The kingdom of God is distinctly different from the world around us. The narrow road does not come naturally to us. It is hard to find and difficult to travel. It is contrary to our inherited inclinations. Travelling on the narrow road requires a lot more sacrifice than most people are willing to make, and it involves a lot more risk than the selfish nature is willing to take. We want to be affirmed and encouraged, not convicted. We want to be entertained, not challenged. We want comfort and safety, not uncertainty and risk. We want answers and assurance, not faith.

Though seeking these things is not natural to our old self, it resonates in the heart of the new self. If the narrow road was simply "being good," more people would find it, but Jesus says that few find it. Finding the narrow road means I must depart from all that comes so naturally and seek the things that I fear, even resent. I must die to myself.

> "As they were walking along the road, a man said to him, 'I will follow you wherever you go.'
>
> Jesus replied, 'Foxes have holes and birds of the air have nests, but the Son of Man has no place to lay his head.'
>
> He said to another man, 'Follow me.'
>
> But the man replied, 'Lord, first let me go and bury my father.'
>
> Jesus said to him, 'Let the dead bury their own dead, but you go and proclaim the kingdom of God.'
>
> Still another said, 'I will follow you, Lord; but first let me go back and say goodbye to my family.'
>
> Jesus replied, 'No one who puts his hand to the plow and looks back is fit for service in the kingdom of God.'"
>
> ~ Luke 9:57-62

Jesus' message to these would-be disciples is that it costs you something — indeed, everything — to be a disciple, a follower of Jesus. The problem in the universal church is that we are still operating in an economy of self. We invite Jesus into our life, to be a part of our life, but we do not grasp the concept that we are to surrender our lives in full to him. He is both Savior and Lord and we are a living sacrifice.

We are called to surrender everything to Jesus. We may not be called to actually give all things up for him, but when we are "buried with Christ in his death," we are saying that we are willing to leave it all behind and follow where he leads. When the Jews brought their offering to the temple, they killed the animal and gave it over, in its entirety, to the priest who burned it on the altar. They could reclaim none of it, yet we feel we must keep parts of our life back for ourselves and we bring an unacceptable offering before God.

Me-ology permeates the church. We read the parable of the soils and assume we are the good soil, even if there is no real evidence to support it. We read the story of Job and assume that we are Job who will be blessed at the end of it all rather than as one of Job's friends who is operating off bad information. Even in our worship songs, hints of the economy of self are evident. Most songs are all about me: "Open the Eyes of *My* Heart," "Meet With *Me*," "*My* All in All," "Every Move *I* Make," "Here *I* Am to Worship." First person songs certainly have their place, and I am not saying it is wrong to sing them. I love some of those songs, but why a first person voice instead of a corporate voice? There are far fewer songs like "How Great is *Our* God," "*We* Fall Down," and "*Everybody* Praise the Lord," written as a part of a whole. In fact, most of the time you see the word "you" in the New Testament, particularly in Paul's letters, it is in the second person plural form of the word, not the singular.

There are many church-going believers who do not live like they trust God. If all we have to go on is what we see of their lives, all we would see is an hour or two of church attendance and a new vocabulary. The Christian life was not meant to be lived with safety nets in place. These are only a hindrance. We cannot trust, obey, and experience God if we only ever do things that we can do on our own, if we are the ones who maintain control of our lives.

I had to come to a point in my own life and ministry where I realized that as long as I avoid obedience and avoid risk I sin and will not see the power, presence, and wonder of God. If, "for the joy set before him" Jesus endured the cross for me, then why can I not endure simple rejection or ridicule for him? If "whoever seeks to save his life will lose it," then many in the church have not known life.

—

> "Not to us, O LORD, not to us but to your name be the glory, because of your love and faithfulness.
>
> Why do the nations say, 'Where is your God?' Our God is in heaven; he does whatever pleases him."
>
> ~ Psalm 115:1-2

We are so concerned with *our* glory. We want to protect *our* reputation, *our* possessions; each of us seeks the approval of men and to preserve *my* safety, hold up *my* priorities, and advance *my* plans. It is no wonder that the world questions, "Where is your God?" Out of fear we fail to trust and obey, and the presence and work of God goes unseen both by us and in us. Faith in Christ appears to be a crutch because that is all we have made it; that is all we expect God to be for us. We want him to be who we want, not who he has promised and revealed himself to be.

God changes the old to new. He transforms. Every person we admire in the scriptures began empty, like dirt; void of value, purpose, and any real meaning. God gave them life and, through adversity, forged and shaped them into someone new and gave them a new name. No one begins as faithful, but rather as an enemy of God. We all have been forgiven far more than we will admit, or know. And we have each been given far more than we can measure by the world's standards.

In Christ we have been made new. We must not simply allow, but seek the change God brings. If there is no change, then we are not surrendered to Christ. Lukewarm is not an option for the one who loves Jesus. In the Sermon on the Mount, Jesus said, "Blessed are they who hunger and thirst for righteousness." All that we seek from our safety nets, worldly possessions, and alternatives to obedience is only found when God himself is our most urgent desire. We will not know safety and security until the storm comes and we witness the faithfulness of God our refuge.

What kind of investments do you make in others? It is not hard to take your spiritual temperature. Do you only reach out to "people like you," people whose needs are not too great, or do you minister to the needs of those who are truly broken and needy? Do you do enough to get by and feel good about yourself, or do you have an unquenchable desire to know God and see the power of his presence in your life? Do you hold back and avoid certain people because, honestly, you're just not willing to invest the time and energy in them, or do you look for opportunities to step out in faith and see God do something that only he can do?

It is easy to assume that God would not do certain things through us. We often use phrases like, "I'm waiting on God," or, "I don't feel led to…" as a way of avoiding the big investments. There are some things you simply do not need to pray about. There are some things that God has already commanded you to do: "Love your neighbor as yourself"; "He who has two tunics, give to he who has none"; "If your enemy is hungry, feed him…" These are not the responsibilities of "super Christians," pastors, elders, or fanatics. We are all called to be fanatics. These are the responsibilities of every follower of Jesus, no exceptions.

It is often said in Christian circles, "God will not give you more than you can handle." This, of course, is poppycock. If God never gave you more than you can handle, then you would never have a need for faith, and most of scripture would then be a lie. God almost always gives you more than you can handle. This way you can experience him in ways you could not without adversity.

God calls us into situations that make us uncomfortable and afraid. Lukewarm Christianity sits safely inside the sheltered harbor of the church building, willing to bend a knee, but unwilling to take up its cross and bear the burden of Jesus' passion. Followers of Jesus love, which always results in sacrifice, and trust him to fill them in their lack.

When Jesus sent out the twelve to the "lost sheep of Israel," he gave them instructions to heal the sick, raise the dead, cleanse the ill, and drive out demons. In other words, they were to engage and invest in those desperately aware of their brokenness and need. Their mission was God-sized and unsafe (and I'm sure a little more than uncomfortable), but they were given a new currency to spend. They were not giving out of their own little coffers. Freely they had received, and out of love and gratitude, they gave just as freely. If we are not making such investments, we are not operating in God's Kingdom economy.

What does it look like to live in a Christ-centered economy? If fear is the currency of the world, then what drives the Kingdom Economy? How do we experience a deeper and more powerful change than simply that of our vocabulary and dress code? Claiming to follow Jesus but clinging to the currency of fear is to settle for less than God's best; we are compromising. In the next chapter, we will see what it looks like to live, not by fear, but by faith.

CHAPTER 3

LIVING IN A KINGDOM ECONOMY

The Currency of the Kingdom

"For God did not give us a spirit of fear, but a spirit of power, of love, and of self-control."
~ 2 Timothy 1:7

The people of God look distinctly different from the rest of the world. One could make a very strong argument that, if that is not the case, then these are not the people of God. In fact, God makes that argument. To the very comfortable church in Laodicea, the Lord says:

> "You say, 'I am rich; I have acquired wealth and do not need a thing.' But you do not realize that you are wretched, pitiful, poor, blind, and naked."
> ~ Revelation 3:17

These words are not used to describe citizens of the Kingdom. These are people who think that temporal comfort is the same as spiritual righteousness. It is clear that they trust in their material wealth more than God and they are rebuked for it. God tells them to sell out and to buy in to his program. In other words, they need to make an economic shift.

God's people know God; they not only believe he exists but trust him to be and do all he has promised. Because of this, God's people don't need all the comforts that the world has to offer. Citizens of the Kingdom process information differently, they respond to challenges differently, and they answer to a different standard. Like salmon swimming upstream, the Christian lives a life that proceeds against the flow of human nature.

While the rest of the world is hiding behind image and temporal trappings, the Christian is free to be who God made them to be, free from any expectation other than those of their Creator. The world lives by a spirit of fear, but the follower of Jesus lives by the power of the Holy Spirit.

If fear is the currency that drives the economy of self, then faith is the currency that drives the economy of the Kingdom. While those lost in "me-first" make their decisions based on fear of what *might* happen, what they *might* lose, or what a particular investment *might* cost them, the child of God makes their decisions with no regard to their own weakness or want. The child of God makes decisions based on who their Father is.

I remember learning to drive as a young teenager. I had a few experiences with motor driven vehicles before – mini bikes, go carts. None of these ended well. Typically, the motor ran off with the vehicle and I was left wounded on the pavement. Now, behind the wheel of a car, I had every reason to be afraid. The motor was bigger, the vehicle was larger and more complicated (and much more expensive), and I had a good list of failures already running through my head. In spite of all this, however, I had confidence. Why? Because I knew I'd get it right this time? No. It was because my dad was right there next to me. I didn't need to have confidence in my ability (or lack thereof). I trusted that my dad would not allow me to fail. Not that I expected to be Mario Andretti on day one (or ever), but my dad knows me, he knows what I need, and he would never set me up to fail. He hadn't yet.

—

Sometimes, it is tempting to doubt God's heart and intent. We demand that he explain himself when we don't understand what is happening, but this is ridiculous. God does not answer to us for anything. We would not even have life, let alone any privilege, without him. He has only proven faithful throughout history. Our enemy wants us to doubt him, but the child of God knows their Father. They default to trust him when things get confusing.

When I was in the Marine Corps, I served as a mortorman in the infantry. We had to handle explosives regularly. I guarantee you, there was healthy fear involved. That fear gave me a healthy respect for the munitions I handled on every live-fire range. You better believe I handled these things with care, but at the same time, I was still able to effectively work with them. My fear of death or dismemberment made me cautious. It did not paralyze me and keep me from doing my job.

Too often, our fears paralyze us and prevent us from fulfilling our purpose. We refuse to invest because of what might happen. Both fear and worry can consume us if we do not identify the threat and keep them in their place. Living your life based on fear and worry is like trying to drive your car by the warning lights in the dashboard. Emotions are indicators, not truths. They are meant to aid us, not dictate our lives. They are important, but not the main event.

—

> "So do not worry, saying, 'What shall we eat?' or 'What shall we drink?' or 'What shall we wear?' For the pagans run after all these things and your heavenly Father knows that you need them."
> ~ Matthew 6:31-32

In the passage above, Jesus tells us that the pagans — those who trust in their own power and ability — run after the things of the world because they are driven by the fear of insignificance and insufficiency. Yet, many in the church still run after all these things also. They know they *should* want God, but their hearts are divided. We believe in God, but we don't necessarily trust him. Just like with Eve in the Garden, the enemy urges us to doubt God's heart, and we buy in. Like the disciples, we ask God, "You do want what's best for *me*, don't you?"

Jesus reminds us that our heavenly Father knows our need. He sees our weakness and brokenness. He accepts us as we are, but refuses to leave us that way. He heals us, fills us, and empowers us to live an abundant life. The process won't always make sense to us, but God wants for you what he knows is best. You want what you *think* is best. To persevere through the process requires faith. We have to trust God to fulfill his promises. The vehicle that drives this Kingdom Economy — the currency of the Kingdom of God — is faith.

> "Now faith is being sure of what we hope for and certain of what we do not see. This is what the ancients were commended for.
>
> By faith we understand that the universe was formed at God's command, so that what is seen was not made out of what is visible.
>
> By faith Abel offered God a better sacrifice than Cain did. By faith he was commended as a righteous man, when God spoke well of his offerings. And by faith he still speaks, even though he is dead.
>
> And without faith it is impossible to please God, because anyone who comes to him must believe that he exists and that he eagerly rewards those who earnestly seek him."
>
> ~ Hebrews 11:1-4, 6

When we live in the Kingdom of God, that is, under the rule and reign of God, our actions are motivated by a very different objective. We recognize that self is far too small a thing for life to be all about and so we look beyond ourselves. We are told that God has revealed his character traits through all he has made. As we look at the world around us, we can see his power, majesty, generosity, and everlasting faithfulness. We see that he is a God of order and of process. We begin to see that God is far greater than all we can know. He is the "more" that we have longed for all our lives. With this revelation comes a desire to know him more.

God has made a very simple but very important promise. He said, "You will seek me and find me when you seek me with all your heart" (Jeremiah 29:13). God wants to be found by you. When you make the commitment to trust him, to surrender your life to him, God will begin to work to reveal himself to you. Unfortunately, we learn best through adversity. When you face a trial, a challenge, or a stressful situation, it is usually because God wants to teach you something about himself. I'm going to guess that, under your own authority, you have experienced your share of failures and harbor more regrets than you would care to admit. God often brings you back to those same kinds of situations in order to demonstrate his faithfulness and power while providing you the opportunity to exhibit faith and grow.

In addition to teaching you something about his character, God also teaches you about yourself through your trials. Going back to the disciples in the boat during the storm on the Sea of Galilee, Jesus wanted to teach them about himself and his divine power. The disciples' response was a question, "Who is this?" Their fear was born out of their ignorance to who Jesus is. They had already been sent out to preach, heal, and drive out demons. They probably were feeling pretty good about themselves. This storm revealed to them that they still had a lot to learn.

We too, are in a process of development. The Bible says "that he who began a good work in you will carry it on to completion until the day of Christ Jesus" (Philippians 1:6). This means that until we go home to eternity, we are in process, so you can expect more joys and trials along the way. It also tells us that it is God who is responsible for the changes that will occur in you. He is sovereign and exercises authority over the events of your life. It is in this reality that the children of God and disciples of Jesus take such great comfort. This truth is what enables you to choose faith rather than fear.

Living in a Kingdom economy is to live beyond what can be seen, heard, touched, tasted, and smelled. We are holistic beings. There is a spiritual element to us. Though the physical element is important, and the part we are most intimately acquainted with, it is still only a part of who we are. We manage the physical and build up the spiritual. The body will die and be made new, but your spirit will endure for eternity — which begins here and now, from the moment you came to trust Jesus for the forgiveness of your sin and for eternal life. The physical is *what* you are; your spirit, or soul, is *who* you are. God is far more concerned with who you are.

Because we know God is sovereign, that he is good, and that he initiates the process of developing who we are, we can have peace in the midst of our trials. To the world, peace is merely the absence of conflict. This, biblically, is an incomplete and shallow definition of peace. How, then, could we have peace in the midst of conflict? No, instead we know that, as it is written, "in all things God works for the good of those who love him and are called according to his purpose" (Romans 8:28). Because we trust him, we can endure and even persevere through trials knowing that we will be better for it in the end.

Perhaps the most liberating truth that you can get your head around is this: God is God, and you are not. Remember, you are dirt, and no one expects dirt to do much of anything. God sees all things and knows all things. Your brokenness and need are not a surprise, and you can never let him down. In fact, he created you, as you are, with all your weaknesses and needs. He did so with a purpose. You were created for dependence. He wants you to want him.

We need to realize that God is complete in and of himself. "God is love." Love is objective. That means that the love shared, one for another, between the Father, the Son, and the Holy Spirit, made God complete without needing anything beyond himself. The point is that God does not *need* you; he *wants* you. You do not have to run around like a chicken with your head cut off striving to get your needs met. You simply need to believe that God is who he says he is and trust that he will do all he has promised. That, in a nut shell, is faith.

Everyone we admire in scripture lived by faith. It was faith, not fear, that guided their actions. Certainly fear was there, looming like a carnie on the midway looking to make a buck, but it didn't control them. What set them apart as exceptional was not their skill set, their intelligence, or their supernatural capacity. It was their willingness to simply trust God. It's what enabled Abel to give his best to God, because he trusted God to provide. It's what enabled Abraham to surrender Isaac, because he trusted God to be faithful to his promise that through Isaac would come a nation. It's what empowered Paul to impact the world for Jesus, because he trusted God to change men's hearts where he could not.

Think about it. Paul was trying to squelch the Christian movement through threat of punishment or death. He trusted in his education, his heritage, his authority, and his zeal. It was not until his encounter with the risen Christ that he was eventually able to "consider everything a loss compared to the surpassing greatness of knowing Christ Jesus my Lord, for whose sake I have lost all things" (Philippians 3:8) and simply trust God. It was only then that he began to really impact the world around him.

—

What allowed faith to flourish in the lives of those in scripture and enabled them to radically change the world around them was not some unique program or special religious ritual; it was a focus on the Father. Rather than holding self as the focus of the economy of their soul, God was there, in his rightful place. He is the reason for our existence, and life works best when it revolves around him.

The economy of self cannot think past its own forehead. It is consumed by the shallow worries and standards of this world and by its own selfish desires. Those who live in the Kingdom economy, however, are free from slavery to the world system. Our focus is so far beyond ourselves that we are not even a factor in the equation. That's the power that belief and trust — faith — can have. It frees us from the trappings of pride. Whether we think too much of our self and fear to lose, or we degrade ourselves and despair, our focus is still on self and we become slaves to pride. With a focus on the Father, we can trust that our needs are both known and accounted for. We need not worry or fear because the One who created all things holds us.

Several years ago, I had won a trip to Hawaii from a local radio station. Part of the trip included a snorkel excursion to Molokini, a partially submerged crater that serves as a very popular snorkel spot. While we were swimming about, one of the guides was collecting marine friends to show us on the boat. Among the critters he was able to collect was a short-spined puffer fish. He, of course, was all swelled up. His puffing up was a defense mechanism to make him harder to swallow, but also to appear as more than he really is. See if you can draw the connection between that and Habakkuk 2:4, which reads:

> "See, he is puffed up; his desires are not upright –
> but the righteous will live by his faith."

The righteous are those in a right relationship with God and who live by the economy of the Kingdom, by faith. They live their lives dependent upon God's goodness and greatness. Those in the world's economy of self make more of themselves than of God and seek their own desires. The context of this verse is that God was telling Habakkuk that Nebuchadnezzar, king of Babylon, was going to come and carry Israel away into captivity as judgment for Israel's sin. Within this pronouncement of judgment is a word of hope, "The righteous shall live by his faith." They would believe and trust God to execute his judgment and also to fulfill his promise of restoration. As a Christian, you live not by what you can make of yourself, but by the person and promises of God.

There are many things beyond our control, and we could spend a great deal of time and energy worrying about them and striving to avoid the inevitable or cover up reality. Those who have surrendered their lives to God and have made the decision to trust him have a different currency to spend. They have faith. Faith and hope are two words that have lost a lot of their punch in our society. They mean to so many something more along the lines of "a wish" or "blind trust." The truth is that there is power in those words. They are what drive the economy of the kingdom.

—

Just as pride and fear drive the economy of self and enslave us, faith and hope drive the economy of the Kingdom and set us free. No longer do we have to protect our fragile but shallow image. No longer are we bound to holding up the world's standards. We are free to be ourselves — who God made us. We are free, not to take and take, feeding the machine, but to give freely of ourselves because we know the One on whom we have believed. Faith makes God more important than "me." Hope is when we look forward to the fulfillment of what God has promised. When we lay aside pride and fear and take up faith and hope, we are relieved of the great burden of making life work — of sustaining life. This is the job of Christ, who "is before all things, and in him all things hold together" (Colossians 1:17).

Pride and fear lead us to worry about the future. Faith and hope allow us to keep an eye on the future, but to be faithful with now, with what is set before us at the moment. Because we trust God, who has proven faithful over the ages, we need not fear or worry about what will be or might be. He is in control, so we do not have to be.

Citizens of the Kingdom are free to invest knowing that the return has eternal value. We rejoice, even in trying times when we are less than happy, because we trust that it is part of the process that is making us "complete and mature, not lacking anything" (James 1:4). We may struggle with fear and doubt, but because of what we know of the Father, we do not let fear and doubt dictate our decisions and attitudes. Our decision to choose faith benefits our own lives, and it also inspires those around us. Just as "one bad apple spoils the bunch," so obedience and faithfulness beget obedience and faithfulness. When we invest freely, we make each other better and contribute to an eternal cycle of eternal value in the lives of others.

An Eternal Return

—

*"I have been reminded of your sincere faith, which first lived
in your grandmother Lois and in your mother Eunice and, I
am persuaded, now lives in you also. For this reason I remind
you to fan into flame the gift of God, which is in you through
the laying on of my hands."*
~ 2 Timothy 1:5-6

"Every man dies, not every man really lives." That is the tag line
for the movie *Braveheart*. If you remember, William Wallace, played
by Mel Gibson, leads the Scottish people in their quest for freedom
from British oppression. We remember the battles, the victories,
and the glories. What we fail to remember (or at least boast about)
is the suffering and sacrifice. William Wallace was a hero, but he
was also a martyr. What he left behind, however, is remembered for
generations. William Wallace's life mattered.

Jesus said, "The thief comes only to steal, kill, and destroy; I have
come that they may have life, and have it to the full" (John 10:10).
There are many things in this world that boast a life lived. In reality,
they steal your life and leave you longing for significance. We spend
our time hiding in video games, on Facebook, or watching television
while life passes us by. We exchange abundant life for virtual living.
Because we drive the right vehicle, wear the right clothes, and have
the right stickers on our truck, we assume we are living the good life,
but we have settled for a fantasy. Fantasy is a substitute for reality.
We have allowed the thief to steal our hopes, kill our heart, and
destroy the life we know we are meant for.

Jesus came to "destroy the devil's work" (1 John 3:8). He came
to take our broken, hollow, fruitless life and exchange it for a rich,
abundant life. He came to turn the spiritual couch potato (or pew
potato if you are a church attendee) into William Wallace.

—

Remember, God is a God of process. Just look at the four seasons
and you can see that God likes ongoing cycles that feed each other
and eventually bear fruit. He is doing the same thing in your life.

Your life is a cycle that is meant to contribute to an even greater cycle that bears fruit long beyond your years.

Timothy, the young man who is named as the recipient of two of Paul's letters recorded in scripture, is a demonstration of what this looks like. Paul refers to Timothy as his "son." Paul mentored Timothy and helped him to grow in his faith and calling. Yet in the second letter to Timothy, Paul gives credit for Timothy's foundation to someone else. He writes, "I have been reminded of your sincere faith, which first lived in your grandmother Lois and in your mother Eunice and, I am persuaded, now lives in you also" (2 Timothy 1:5).

Notice that the investment of Timothy's grandmother had an impact on Timothy's mother. The two of them together laid a foundation in Timothy's life as they connected him to Christ. Paul was then able to build on that foundation. Eventually, Timothy was appointed as pastor of the church in Ephesus where he was used by God, through his investments of himself, in the development of those we call the early church fathers.

It is possible that Lois, Timothy's grandma, was the first generation believer in that family, but look at the harvest her faith produced. That is "good soil." That is significance. Timothy's father is hardly mentioned. Apparently, he did not make an investment and therefore yielded no return. We know that Timothy's father was a Greek. Beyond that, we know nothing of him. That is insignificance.

—

Perhaps the greatest longing in the human heart is for significance. We want to know that we matter, that our lives make a difference. The world offers us opportunities to make an impression, but seldom a difference. We can make a statement with the clothes we wear, we can make a reputation through the donations we make to charity, and we can develop an image through our accomplishments. Yet all of these avenues both begin and end with "me." Once I come to an end, my statements, reputation, and image fade away with me. As we have covered earlier, you are too small a thing for life to be all about.

Life is more than being born and dying and doing the best you can in between. That is existence. We were created to *live*.

Even inanimate living things leave a legacy. Disney's *The Lion King* even caught on to that one. They talked about the circle of life, a cycle of interdependence where the lives of living things contribute to the life and survival of other living things. Humans are really the only creatures who don't get that concept. We were made to contribute to a bigger picture. Unless we are part of a whole, we will remain insignificant and unfruitful.

God's purpose was for more than mere survival, more than mere existence, more than simply attending church. His purpose was one of intention, of life, and of prosperity. This cannot happen when our lives are lived in a bubble. It requires relationships, and relationships require investment.

—

Relationship is at the very heart of the Gospel of God. It is only through healthy, Christ-centered relationships that we can find and fulfill our purpose and leave an eternal legacy of eternal value. At the inception of the nation of Israel, God commanded his people:

> "Keep [God's] decrees and commands, which I am giving you today, so that it may go well with you and your children after you and that you may live long in the land the LORD your God gives you for all time."
>
> ~ Deuteronomy 4:40

And as Joshua was getting ready to lead the people across the Jordan River to take the Promise Land:

> "Be strong and very courageous. Be careful to obey all the law that my servant Moses gave you; do not turn from it to the right or the left, that you may be successful wherever you go."
>
> ~ Joshua 1:7

God has given us his law for our good. He wants us to live prosperous lives. This is not the fallacy of the health, wealth, and prosperity gospel. This is not Joel Osteen or Benny Hinn telling you that God wants you to have a fat bank account, a fancy car, a successful career, and a perfect bill of health. There is no give-money-to-some-preacher-and-God-will-bless-you magic formula. That thinking destroys the faith of those in seasons of trial and suffering.

The law God is referring to is the Torah, the teachings. All the commands of the Old Testament Law can be summed up in the Ten Commandments. Those ten, as Jesus said, can be summed up in two great commands — offered as one single command:

> "Love the Lord your God with all your heart, with all your soul, with all your mind, and with all your strength. The second is this: Love your neighbor as yourself. There is no commandment greater than these."
>
> ~ Mark 12:30-31

> "All the Law and the Prophets hang on these two commands."
>
> ~ Matthew 22:40

The law that we are to keep in order to live long and fruitful lives, lives that make a difference, lives that matter, is that of relationship. We are to first live in a right relationship with God and second, in a right relationship with others. Love God; love others. That is what all the commands we fret over come down to. When we read about how the Israelites were not supposed to wear blended fabrics, we are reading about the command to remain pure and exclusive. What they did — what we do — in the temporal affects who they were — who we are — in the spiritual, and vice versa.

Remember, we are holistic beings. We cannot deal with parts of who and what we are to the neglect of the other parts. It's all connected. Paul wrote to the church in Rome, "Offer your bodies as living sacrifices, holy and pleasing to God — this is your spiritual act of worship" (Romans 12:2). The acts of the body and the condition of our spirit are connected. Your relationship with God may be built internally, but it must be lived externally. Faith must be lived outside the confines of our private lives. This is unsafe, risky, perhaps even dangerous, but it is required if we are to be a William Wallace to lives enslaved by fear and lies.

—

Worship is a simple word, but a complex concept. In the Greek it means to bow down. In the Hebrew, there are different words for worship which involve almost every aspect of life. Whether by definition or through context, worship is more than any single act. It is a life lived unto God.

We can worship many different things. When we live for something other than God, whether it is self, our kids, our stuff, a reputation or image, power and position, a thing, a person, or a concept, we offer ourselves in worship to that thing. True worship is not the pursuit of the temporal. It is the pursuit of God.

God reveals himself through what he has made, through his written word, through the person of Jesus Christ, through the activity of the Holy Spirit, through his children, and in many other ways. True worshippers are those who receive that revelation and respond. That response can be prayer, praise, singing, crying, falling prostrate; it can be brokenness, joy, peace; we can express it through joyful noise, or reverent silence. We can worship by ourselves, in a group, at home, at work, or as we go about any number of daily chores. Worship is virtually unlimited, and we are commanded to worship God. In fact, it is impossible to foster a relationship with him without worship.

Worship fosters a healthy relationship with God and encourages our relationships with others. In worship we find common ground — unity. In worship we encourage, confess, and discover. It comes as no surprise that worship is most effective when it is done in relationship with our brothers and sisters in Christ. Gifted musicians, singers, speakers, prayer warriors, administrators, leaders, and honest and sincere hearts come together to bring a bigger picture of worship than one could bring alone. Worship also leads us to serve one another.

Worship, essentially, is a service to God. It is our way of giving back to the One who has everything. As we respond to his revelation of himself, others benefit and we are filled. God reveals himself and fills us with each encounter. This equips us to, in turn, give to those around us. "Freely you have received, freely give" (Matthew 10:8). Complete and proper worship of God will bless someone else. In this, God is pleased.

—

We were created in God's image. Our purpose is to know God and make God known. When we grow to truly know God, as the heart and mind of Christ is formed in us by the Holy Spirit through our experiences (good, bad, and otherwise), and we begin to live from that heart, we reflect, or resemble, God. People who do not know God begin to encounter him through our lives lived for him.

As we fulfill the purpose of God in this way, our lives take on an eternal meaning. We become full and fruitful. Our lives matter and we make a difference. Often we can wonder if this is true. I know I certainly do. I, too, long for significance. Like you, I wonder if I am really doing enough. Then, I get an email like this one:

"Yesterday was a fabulous, very special day for me! I just want to thank you and Mike again (as I thank God for you every day) for sticking by me, being patient with me, not judging me, and just for playing such an important role in helping me get back on the right track and back into God's loving hands. It's so amazing how only 2 or 3 months ago, I felt kind of "out of place" at church and around congregants, and now it's my favorite place to be! I'm like those boys you told us about yesterday...all week I'm asking God, "Is it Sunday yet?" LOL And when I wouldn't have given prayer a second thought (or I would only pray when I wanted something) a few months ago, now I spend a great deal of time IN prayer...constant communication with my Creator! I love it, I love Him, and I love you and your family! Thank you so much."

This is an excerpt from a note my wife and I received from a long-time friend. We had known Anne Marie since before we were walking with Christ. Before we were married, we were living for ourselves, driven by fear and selfish desire; we had no effect in her life. We were friends and fellow partiers. When God changed Tricia and I, and began forging us into the likeness of his Son, it was then we were make a lasting difference in someone's life.

This email came to us in August of 2004. In July of '04, Anne Marie and her husband Nick were one signature away from divorce. Today, Anne Marie has been reconciled to her husband and they have become an important part of our church fellowship. She has, for two years now, served on our leadership team as the Worship Ministry Team leader. Her husband Nick serves as a deacon and runs the A/V booth on Sundays and during the mid-week. You see, God changed my wife and me, and then used us to impact Anne Marie's life. Together, we were used in Nick's life and now they are impacting the lives of others. No special methods or programs. In fact, I can't even really remember any special ritual or particular investment. We were just living out of the heart that God had formed in us and investing in those around us. We worshipped him in our relationships, and a life was transformed.

This is not to say that I always get it right. Please, I'll pass on the pedestal. But that is the beauty of a living relationship with God. He takes both our victories and failures and uses them in the process of our development. When we remain open to what God shows us, we remain teachable, moldable, and useful. God has established a covenant, not a contract. A contract sets terms and limits, which, if violated, nullify the contract. A covenant also sets boundaries, but when they are crossed or terms violated, the covenant remains and we grow stronger through the process of reconciliation. You do not become useless, nor are you rejected when you fail. You get convicted, corrected, and remain cherished. Through your failures you become even more useful when you allow God to teach you.

Pride will thwart efforts to change. We may not think we need to change. But change — uncertain and frightening as it may be

— is necessary. All living things grow, develop, and mature — they change. To resist change is to resist life. Though you may find yourself uncertain of the coming changes, you can remain certain of God who is both great and good. It is in him we place our trust and find peace. It is in him we discover our purpose and realize the meaning of our lives. It is in right relationship with God lived out among others that we find significance and leave an eternal legacy.

Chapter 4

Turning the Economy Around

Establishing Healthy Credit

-

"For by the grace given me I say to each one of you: Do not
think of yourself more highly than you ought, but rather
think of yourself with sober judgment, in accordance with the
measure of faith God has given you."
~ Romans 12:3

If what we suffer from is an unhealthy, over-inflated view of self,
then the cure is to grasp a humble — or realistic — view of self.
When we were first married, my wife and I both worked and were
able to make ends meet. We, like so many others, wanted more than
to just get by, so we began to supplement our lifestyle through credit
cards. When we ran the balance up, another offer came in the mail.
We would pay down the first one and run the balance up on the new
one. Eventually, reality caught up with us.

When the transmission on our car failed, we had to use the first
credit card to afford the repairs. Now we had two credit cards with
limits maxed out and insufficient income to pay them down. We
could make the minimum payments, but could never seem to gain
any ground. We looked prosperous on the outside, but in the end
we were only rich in debt.

We have all tapped our resources, living on bogus credit that we will never be able to pay off. We need a wake-up call if we are going to be brought to a place where God can do his work in and through us. Since we are all different, that jolt into reality will differ. Some need a gentle nudge, while others require something more significant.

You are dirt. That may sound like drill instructor jargon, but it's biblical. Dirt is the basic building block. It's what we need to get back to. Think about it. What astrologers refer to as "star-stuff" and biologists call "basic building blocks" is the foundational material from which all matter is derived. Scientists think this realization points to evolution, but it really supports what the Bible teaches. Scripture says, "So God created man from the dust of the ground and breathed into his nostrils the breath of life, and the man became a living being" (Genesis 2:7). Additionally, God tells Adam at the curse, "For dust you are and to dust you will return" (Genesis 3:19). The fact remains, you and I are dirt.

The good news is that God loves dirt. God took you (dirt) and gave you life. He has given you gifts, talents, abilities, and purpose. Apart from God you are just dirt wallowing through mere existence. No God, no purpose — no meaning. It is God who has given dirt (you) life and value and purpose. The sooner we embrace and delight in this reality, the sooner we will realize abundant and productive life.

—

Think back on what you know about the Beatitudes. We can all remember the "Blessed are…" part, but what was Jesus really saying? Let's look at his message. The first step is to develop a healthy perspective.

> "Blessed are the poor in spirit, for theirs is the kingdom of heaven.
> Blessed are those who mourn, for they will be comforted.

Blessed are the meek (or humble), for they will inherit the earth.

Blessed are those who hunger and thirst for righteousness, for they will be filled."

~ Matthew 5:3-6

What Jesus is describing is a process of transformation. He is showing his audience, and all who would later take the time to read these words, how to make the shift in their spiritual economy from an empty and fruitless economy of self to a vibrant and productive life of value, meaning, and purpose.

This process begins with a shift in how we see ourselves. The poor in spirit are those who come to recognize their brokenness and need and admit that they bring nothing to the table – like a new recruit on day one of Boot Camp. The poor in spirit embrace the fact that they are dirt and, alone, can only make things dirty. It is at this point that the kingdom of heaven opens to us, for, "Though the LORD is on high, he looks upon the lowly, but the proud he knows from afar" (Psalm 138:6).

Once we recognize our broken condition, those who mourn that brokenness find comfort in God's grace. It is one thing to acknowledge your sin and failure, but quite another to mourn it. Think back to a time when a friend, girlfriend, maybe even a spouse betrayed your trust. Think how painful that was. This is what we have done to God. That should bother us. If you have ever heard someone who has supposedly encountered the saving grace of God talk about their life of rebellion as if they are proud of it (and maybe even miss it), they clearly do not mourn their brokenness. It is when we are grieved that we have missed the mark and broken our relationship with God that we find comfort in God's grace. Otherwise, it's little more than fire insurance.

The Greek word πραεις can be translated as "meek" but is better translated "humble" (which is very much the same spirit as meekness). Pride tells us that we can manage on our own, that we can make things better and earn our way back to favor with God and others. Pride says, "I can fix this." Humility realizes the need for something beyond self. Those who have come to realize and accept their brokenness and need, who mourn that condition and the effect it has had on their relationship with God and others can only find healing and hope through humility: a willingness to receive from God what only he can give you. Through humility, we take God at his word and trust him. It is through this trust (faith) in God's intervention that we can find adoption as children of God and receive an inheritance. "For it is by grace that you are saved, through faith — and this is not of yourselves, it is the gift of God — not by works so that no one can boast" (Ephesians 2:8-9).

This process of brokenness has an intriguing effect on you. It makes you want more. Any addiction that the world offers, whether it is drugs and alcohol, sex, smoking, or video games and Facebook, will only take and take, leaving you empty, unfulfilled, and ineffective. You were created to need God. You find significance and meaning in him only. Every other addiction is a destructive counterfeit. God is what you need. It's the difference between being addicted to crack cocaine and being addicted to air. As the song says, "this is the air I breathe…this is my daily bread." God gives life; everything else — when not kept in its proper place — will take life.

When you hunger and thirst for God, you just can't get enough. The more you know, the more you want to know. The more you experience, the more you want to experience. You can't stop thinking about him, talking about him, or praying to him. He becomes your heartbeat. As it is written:

> "Trust in the LORD with all your heart and do not lean on your own understanding; in all your ways acknowledge him, and he will make your paths straight. Do not be wise in your own eyes; fear the LORD and shun evil. This will bring health to your body and nourishment to your bones."
>
> ~ Proverbs 3:5-8

The one who will prosper and find significance (and is able to lead others to do likewise) is the one who can't get enough of God, who depends upon God and surrenders to God at every occasion, every decision, every need, and every hope. When God permeates a life, that life is powerful and effective and inspires those around them, encouraging them toward God.

In the economy of self, good deeds and generosity are offered for gain. We give with the hope of gaining something down the road. The Bible calls this "selfish ambition." The second step of God's process gives us, through our new, healthy perspective, a healthy motivation to drive our actions.

> "Blessed are the merciful, for they will be shown mercy.
>
> Blessed are the pure in heart, for they will see God.
>
> Blessed are the peacemakers, for they will be called children of God."
>
> ~ Matthew 5:7-9

Jesus moves from hungering and thirsting for more of God to, "Blessed are the merciful." You see, as we go through this process we begin to see others from the same humble perspective. We are able to see that they, too, are broken and wounded and in need of God's redeeming mercy and grace. Those who truly encounter God's mercy toward them are more willing to offer it to those around them — even if we feel they do not deserve it — because we realize that we didn't deserve it either. Mercy is a two-way street. As we show it, we show that we *know* it and have received it.

No longer are decisions driven by fear, selfish ambition, and the deceitful lure of comfort and ease, but rather from a pure heart — one that earnestly seeks the best interest of the other person. To be pure in heart is to operate from the desire to please God. Through that motive, God is revealed and we can see him at work in, through, and around us. God will still use deeds done from selfish motives. The difference is that we miss the blessing because we are still focused on "me." We see the glory of God when the focus is on God.

Our honest and humble desire for the common good — the good of others — drives our desire to make peace. Making peace is much more than merely eliminating conflict. In fact, making peace often causes conflict.

This raises the question, "What is peace?" Peace must be more than an absence of conflict if we can have peace in the midst of conflict. Jesus sure seemed to cause conflict. So did his disciples and apostles. It is written that people accused them of "causing trouble all over the world" (Acts 17:6). So what were they doing? They were challenging people to get right with God. Just like a bookkeeper has to point out overspending, or a doctor has to diagnose the disease, it is a necessary first step if we are to realize healing, hope, and freedom.

Peace is a restored order. When we surrender to God as Lord and he has his rightful place as first in our lives, everything else prospers. It is through faith in him that we have peace when we can see no reason to. Therefore, to make peace is to restore right order from the chaos of our lives, and then in the lives of those around us. This is what Jesus came to do; it is the will of the Father, and the work of the Holy Spirit. When we partner with God in this endeavor, we are doing the things God himself would do; we bear the family resemblance and are "called children of God."

—

All of this change will not go unnoticed. As we have said, no one likes to be wrong. No one wants to hear the waiter say, "I'm sorry, sir. The bank has refused this card." When the world experiences the conviction that comes from witnessing a life well lived in the presence of God, they will resist, even fight it. This is why we love the tabloids. We can build people up to celebrity status — even those who don't deserve it, like Paris Hilton and Jon and Kate Gosslin — and then we watch them fall, or tear them down, and we can feel better about ourselves. We celebrate the failures of others to lift ourselves up. When someone truly prospers and lives in the favor of God, the world will look to tear them down to hide their own hurt and guilt and shame. It's called persecution, and it is why we need to develop a healthy passion.

"Blessed are those who are persecuted because of righteousness, for theirs is the kingdom of heaven.

Blessed are you when people insult you, persecute you and falsely say all kinds of evil against you because of me. Rejoice and be glad, because great is your reward in heaven, for in the same way they persecuted the prophets who were before you."

~ Matthew 5:10-12

The word "passion" usually stirs in us an image of deeply invested love…or lust. The word has another meaning. It means, to suffer. Most of our passions are a lust for temporal things we can collect and control. The passion of Christ is for you. He does not need you, he wants you. He wants you so bad it hurts; he suffers for want of your love and devotion. Passion for things is an endless suffering. Things will never satisfy. The treasure of heaven — relationships, first with God and then with others — is all that will fulfill us. That is something to live for. Without a healthy passion, persecution will break our spirit. Like the seed that fell on shallow soil or among the weeds in Jesus' parable of the sower in Matthew 13, we will grow and seem to flourish in good times, but unmet expectations and simple trials will cause us to wither and shrink back.

Persecution is a part of the process. It is the acid test of devotion. Notice that Jesus doesn't say "if" you are persecuted, but "when" you are persecuted. It is also important to note the reason for the persecution. He says, "because of righteousness," and "because of me." When someone is just rude to you, that is not persecution. If you're a selfish jerk, it is not persecution when people avoid you or tell you off. Remember, the Gospel is, by nature, offensive. You must not be.

Persecution comes when we live from a healthy perspective of self and a healthy motive for the good of others as God, the Author of life, defines it. That is when people encounter the truth of Jesus Christ in your words, actions, and attitudes. It isn't hard to profess faith when faith is accepted. When it costs you something, then we see what you're made of. *Foxe's Book of Martyrs* contains story after story of God's children who endured torture and death because they would not deny their Lord nor forsake the humble life of love for God and others to which they were called.

One such story is that of Immanuel Andegeresgh and Kibrom Firemichel. On October 17, 2006 in Eritrea, a small country-state on the northern border of Ethiopia, these two men sought to worship their Savior. Though they knew it was against the law, their hunger and thirst to meet with God through fellowship and worship was too great. During the worship service, uniformed police crashed in on the meeting, arrested Immanuel, Kibrom, and eight others, and took them off to be imprisoned and tortured. In military confinement, Immanuel (23) and Kibrom (30) died of dehydration and injuries received at the hands of their captors. That kind of selfless sacrifice — that investment in the Kingdom — cannot be made unless the process is real. You can't fake that. Faith must drive your decisions when you "face death all day long…like sheep to be slaughtered" (Romans 8:36).

—

To make the economic shift, we first need all three of these personal transformations: a healthy perspective, a healthy motivation, and a healthy passion. Though we have built up debt in the form of compromises and counterfeits which has buried our hearts in fear, God has made available debt relief. When we recognize the emptiness of what we have built, the severity of our poor investments, and the illusion of self-made security and surrender our heart, mind, soul, and strength to God — committing to live his way — we begin to live from God's credit line.

When we trust in our own ability, we trust in a source of credit that comes with no guarantee. When we live from God's provision, we find a greater resource than we can ever exhaust. Look again at God's gracious words to his church and see the contrast between the riches of self, and the riches of God.

> "You say, 'I am rich; I have acquired wealth and
> do not need a thing.' But you do not realize that
> you are wretched, pitiful, poor, blind, and naked. I

counsel you to buy from me gold refined in the fire,
so you may become rich; and white clothes to wear
so you can cover your shameful nakedness; and
salve to put on your eyes so you can see."

~ Revelation 3:17-18

Comfort and ease are the foundation of shifting sand. These feelings change with every circumstance. What God offers is an eternal and stable, unchanging alternative to what the world can offer. Before we can impact the world around us, we have to settle the debts within us first. It must begin with you. "For it is time for judgment to begin with the family of God. And if it begins with us, what will the outcome be for those who do not obey the gospel of God?" (1 Peter 4:17) The Lord your God has so much more for you than what you have settled for. Are you ready to see yourself for who you really are, to offer your life to God, and experience full and abundant life as he works his purpose in and through you?

Exchanging Your Currency

—

"Therefore, if anyone is in Christ, he is a new creation; the
old has gone, the new has come."
~ 2 Corinthians 5:17

I've heard a couple preachers go out on a limb to suggest a possible method for how the Egyptians enslaved the Israelites after Joseph died. They suggest that as Israel grew more prosperous and wealthy in their little corner of Egypt and as the new Pharaoh grew more afraid of them, he devised a plan to change the currency of the Egyptian economy. When Egyptians came to exchange currency, they traded straight across, but when the sons of Israel came, they changed the exchange rate to favor Egypt. The Israelites incurred so much debt in the transition that they had to go into slavery to settle their debts. It was an advantage that Egypt would not relinquish until Moses — when God delivered the people.

There is no valid way to confirm that theory, but it certainly illustrates what needs to happen in our own lives. We need to shift the economy of our soul from one of self to an economy of Christ and exchange our currency of fear for a currency of faith. Only then will we see our lives reclaimed for the kingdom and endowed with power to fulfill God's purpose. In this exchange we are confronted with our debt and our inability to pay it. Yet God fills our account from the riches of his grace and we find ourselves, not *re*newed, but made new, and unlike the possible exchange in Egypt, God's exchange does not bring slavery, but freedom and fulfillment.

—

Though God works a transition in you personally, it does not end there. There is another transition that takes place. The original covenant with Abraham was that God would bless him, and he would in turn be a blessing to the nations. Unfortunately, due to suffering the consequences of their rebellion (a rebellion driven by the fear that God wasn't enough, just to note), they turned inward and sought only their own righteousness. Once we exchange our currency of fear for a currency of faith, we must again transition from an economy focused on self to an economy focused on God which is manifest in concern for others.

The first step in this transition is to see God for who he is. That might seem elementary. You may be tempted to skim over this section thinking that you know God already, but there are two places most Christians settle and both are dangerous.

The first counterfeit is to know *about* God. A little information is a dangerous thing. Remember when Jesus said that there were many people who were religiously successful who would say, "Lord, Lord," as if they were on God's short-list. Jesus' response to these who knew a lot about God and religion was, "I never knew you. Away from me you evildoers!" (Matthew 7:23)

The second place is more of a compromise. Many Christians know God in a capacity limited by their own experiences, feelings, and thoughts and are content to tarry in their journey thinking they have enough of God. That is like getting to hear a 30 min. sermon by Billy Graham once a week on the radio, but turning down the opportunity to actually meet him, spend time with him at his house and pick his brain. Of course we would jump at the opportunity to get close and personal with the people we admire and hope to emulate. Why would it be any less when it comes to God? He wants this for you. He wants you to live a life of discovery as you draw closer and closer to him each day, each moment.

God's desire for you is so great that the entire Bible declares this one command. The most important — the greatest commandment, the one thing we absolutely must get — is spelled out for us by Jesus:

> "The most important [commandment],' answered Jesus, 'is this: 'Hear O Israel, the Lord your God, the Lord is one. Love the Lord your God with all your heart, all your soul, all your mind, and all your strength.' The second is this: 'Love your neighbor as yourself.' There is no greater commandment than these.

"Well said teacher,' the man replied. 'You are right in saying that God is one and there is no other but him. To love him with all your heart, with all your understanding and with all your strength, and to love your neighbor as yourself is more important than all burnt offerings and sacrifices.'

"When Jesus saw that he had answered wisely, he said to him, 'You are not far from the kingdom of God.'"

~ Mark 12:29-34

How much better must it be to hear, "You are not far from the kingdom," rather than, "Get away from me?" What sets this young scribe apart from his contemporaries or the people in Jesus example? He was willing to see God for who he is, not through the little theological box of his day. Also, he understood what all the religion was supposed to mean.

If life is to be lived and eternal life realized, then we need to grasp and apply this two part foundation. We know there is power in it because it does not begin, in any way, with us. As all things should, it begins with God. Our very lives begin with God. He is, "the Alpha and the Omega; the Beginning and the End; the First and the Last" (Revelation 1:8, 2:8, 21:6). Everything begins and ends with God. We are dirt, remember, and the only thing that gives us power, purpose, meaning, value, even life, is God. This single and greatest commandment begins, not with instruction, but with a declaration. "Hear O Israel, the Lord your God, the Lord is one."

We usually want the short list. "Just tell me what I need to do and let's get on with it." Like the rich young ruler who asked Jesus, "Teacher, what must I do to inherit eternal life" (Mark 10:17), we just want our fire insurance policy. But that is not what this is about. It is about God.

We are told in Hebrews that "Without faith it is impossible to please God" (Hebrews 11:6). Faith is defined in the same letter as "being sure of what we hope for, and certain of what we do not see" (Hebrews 11:1). In other words, faith is a belief that God is who he says he is, and a trust that he can, and will, do all he has promised. Faith begins with a knowledge of God, however limited that may be. Since faith — saving faith — affects our actions, obedience to God must also begin with an understanding of who God is. The more we know God, the more we will love him. The more we love God, the more eager we are to trust him and obey him. As we follow in obedience, we grow to know him more, which continues the cycle of spiritual growth.

After holding up the person of God, Jesus then gives us our first action step. You are to "Love the Lord your God with all your heart, with all your soul, with all your mind, and with all your strength." In other words, love God with every fiber of your being. It is easy to gloss over this, breeze past it, "Love God. Check. I love God." But if I really think about it, can I say I love God with *all* my heart, soul, mind, and strength? Sure, I love God with my mind…most of the time. I love him with *all* my heart…often enough. I love him with most of my heart darn near all of the time. In reality however, I think we would all have to confess that first part is a tall, tall order to which none of us measures up.

Then there is the question, "Do I really love God, or do I merely know and agree that it is something I *should* do and so I've just developed some rituals and habits that seem like love?" That brings us back to the young scribe's response to Jesus' lesson. It seems clear from the scriptures that though Jesus did not ask a question that solicited a response, a response seemed commonly accepted since Jesus "saw that he answered wisely." Both in that time and culture, and in ours today, to rephrase a statement is a good demonstration of listening, thinking, and absorbing a teaching. His answer was that love of God, and so of others, is more important than burnt offerings and sacrifices. Love is far superior to, and more important than, religious habits and rituals and traditions. Love for God is revealed as an unquenchable desire for God.

When courting my wife, I couldn't spend too much time with her. I hung on her every word and went to great lengths — sacrifice — to give her what she needed and wanted. I listened intently to her, served her with great joy, would rearrange my schedule to make time for her, and even risk damaging other friendships in order to nurture my relationship with her. Have I ever loved God that way? I can't seem to focus in my prayer times. My mind wanders as I study his word. More often than I'd like to admit, I struggle to make time to meet with God in a "quiet time." Am I willing to risk damaging a human relationship for the sake of my love for God? Sometimes I have to confess that I fear men and look to please people over God. And I bet you do too if you're really honest. We play church because it looks good and is easier than being real.

We begin with who God is because it is there that we begin to understand how much God first loved us. Again, it begins with God. This is the first part of our basic purpose: Know God.

—

We would not even know what love is or how to love one another had God not first loved us. The love of God led to the sacrifice which overcame sin and death. Our love, in this fear-based economy of self, struggles to overcome the fear of rejection.

Paul wrote to the churches in Rome, "Love must be sincere." This is essential given the nature of love. Godly love, true love, is sacrificial. It is objective, keeping as its focus the best interest of the loved over that of the lover. This reality blows us away. When a marriage goes sour, we say, "They fell out of love." What we really mean when we say, "I don't love you anymore," is that "I am not getting what I expect out of this relationship anymore." That is not love. That is part of the "me-first" economy of self.

When we encounter, are filled, and are moved by God's love, the natural result is a pouring out of that love to others. What seems like a second commandment, "Love your neighbor as yourself," is actually just the other side of the same coin. When we see God for who he is and understand the depth and magnitude of his love, we are compelled to love him back. Since this love is foreign to my natural self, I have to learn and grow into it. As I do, God's perfect love will impact the love I have for others. To be redeemed unto God is to be redeemed into his body, the church, and thus to others.

How do we know when God's love truly has a hold of us? When our love for others begins to look more and more like the love we naturally have for ourselves. This is less about a ritualistic 50/50 split. It is more about wanting as much for someone else as you are inclined to want for yourself.

There was a man in our church named Don. Don was homeless, unemployed, and an alcoholic. He had known better times, but now all he had was a longing for more. I too wanted more for him. I was able to take time for him, pray with him, offer him counsel, and meet some basic needs. Over time, Don began to grow in his understanding of how God had been at work in his life. He began to learn how to be loved and began to get his life back as he lived from who God said he was rather than the lies he'd been hearing all his life. Now, Don is eager to be a witness and a testimony to others, to help the broken in their need. He has learned to receive love, and also how to love others as he himself is loved. This transition in how you think about and perceive your relationship to others is what facilitates your impact on a broken world.

—

We have already discussed God's process for your personal transformation, where he leads you to a healthy perspective of self, a healthy motive for your actions, and a healthy passion that keeps you going. All this is not merely to make you a better person. God is a big-picture God. In fact, as Jesus continues his teaching in the Sermon on the Mount, he adds:

> "You are the salt of the earth. But if the salt loses its saltiness, how can it be made salty again? It is no longer good for anything but to be thrown out and trampled by men.

> "You are the light of the world. A city on a hill cannot be hidden. Neither do people light a lamp and put it under a bowl. Instead they put it on its stand, and it gives light to everyone in the house. In the same way, let your light shine before men, that they may see your good deeds and praise your Father in heaven.

> "Do not think I have come to abolish the Law and
> the Prophets; I have not come to abolish them but
> to fulfill them. I tell you the truth, until heaven and
> earth disappear, not the smallest letter, nor the least
> stroke of a pen, will disappear from the Law until
> everything is accomplished."
>
> ~ Matthew 5:13-18

In our capitalist economy, each individual investor is a small but important part of the bigger picture. The actions of the few can impact the whole market as we influence trends and market forecasts. When you cling to your hard-earned dollars, the market weakens. When you spend, the market begins to flourish. In the same way, when you reserve yourself and let everyone fend for themselves, community suffers. Your family suffers, your workplace suffers, your church suffers, and your neighborhood suffers when you hold out on them out of self-preservation (which, by the way, is driven by fear). When you trust God and invest in others by spending your time, talents, and treasure to encourage, support, and hold them accountable, the whole — whether family, work, church, or community — will flourish. You have the power, in Christ, to make a significant difference in the world around you.

The truth of it is you were not saved by God's grace simply for your own sake. As Jesus said, "No one lights a lamp and puts it under a bowl." God did not put his light in you for no reason. Your new life extends beyond yourself, and the above passage reveals how you plug in and boost the spiritual economy of our failing world. Your personal relationship with God is meant to have a public impact.

—

You may notice as you search the scriptures that God is much less concerned with what you do and much more concerned with who you are. The reason for this is that who you are will affect your decisions and your actions — what you do. As God's process for your personal transformation begins to take root, it will begin to change the way you see the world around you, the way you process information, the way you view various circumstances, and how you respond to the barrage of stimuli that you receive every day. This is your personal influence.

If you scan Paul's first letter to Timothy and his letter to Titus, you will note that he outlines the qualifications for leadership within the church. Notice that there is no list of duties; rather, Paul lists character traits. Your position of leadership, of influence, is determined by who you are. When you are grounded in a right relationship with God, having a realistic — humble — view of self and utterly dependent on and surrendered to him, you can then influence others. Those who are still influenced by the mindset of the world system are no good to anyone. They are "tossed back and forth like a wave of the sea" (James 1:6).

Jesus said that his disciples are the "salt of the earth." Though we can piecemeal an explanation together for this, it's real meaning is somewhat veiled to our modern western minds. Jacob Milgrom, a Jewish scholar, noted that salt was present in the animal sacrifices as well as the grain offerings. We often presume that the salt is a preservative and flavor additive, but Milgrom goes deeper and draws a contrast between salt, which was commanded, and leaven, which was forbidden. Leaven, or yeast, initiates change, where salt is a preservative which represents permanence. A "salt covenant," then, is a permanent unbreakable agreement between God and man. As salt of the earth, you are a symbol of that irrevocable covenant.

Therefore, when Jesus makes his statement that salt cannot be made salty again, it serves the same purpose as the statement made in Hebrews 6:

> "It is impossible for those who have once been enlightened, who have tasted the heavenly gift, who have shared in the Holy Spirit, who have tasted the goodness of the word of God and all the powers of the coming age, if they fall away, to be brought back to repentance, because to their loss they are crucifying the Son of God all over again and subjecting him to public disgrace."
>
> ~ Hebrews 6:4-6

These statements were never intended to spark a debate on whether we can lose our salvation or not. These words were spoken to a people steeped in the Old Testament sacrificial system. They could go to temple, offer their sacrifice and be deemed forgiven, then go back to their lives to live as they want because they knew they could go back and offer another sacrifice to cover their sin. In Christ, it is not this way.

God's process of transformation makes you a new creation. As the scripture says, "you were bought at a price" (1 Corinthians 6:20). In other words, Jesus is Lord. You are to surrender your life to him, not invite him into your life. You are no longer your own. As salt of the earth, you stand for the covenant that God has purchased your freedom from the world's economy with the blood of Jesus Christ. He has taken over your account, settled your debts, and infused your failing life with his credit. This is who you are: His child. You either are, or you are not. There is no sitting on the fence, there is no turning back. As the apostle John observed, "They went out from us, but they did not really belong to us. For if they had belonged to us, they would have remained with us; but their going showed that none of them belonged to us" (1 John 2:19). You are in, or you are out.

Those who are in, who have taken that step of faith, surrendered to the lordship of Christ, and who are following him, will live their lives in such a way that people take notice. Salt that has lost its saltiness is trampled by men, falling under foot as they go about their busy, but fruitless, lives. Good salt is of high value. Roman soldiers were often paid in salt (hence the expression "worth your salt"). Good salt gains the attention of those lost in the day to day, the same way a one hundred dollar bill on the sidewalk does to us. They see the value of it and desire it. Live your life in such a way that you declare the value, worth, and joy of God's covenant to those you encounter each day as you encourage and inspire them. As an individual, that is how your personal influence works.

—

Much to the surprise of many, the church is not a trophy case where we clean ourselves, put on the polish and put ourselves on display. The church is a tool shed into which God will reach in order to transform others and change the world. Whether the tools are hammers, saws, and pliers or calculators, balance sheets, and mechanical pencils, we are here to be used for the common good and we need to be available to the Master to invest in those around us. We are redeemed to make a public investment.

Jesus said that "A city on a hill cannot be hidden." In other words, you cannot hide what you are. If you are a child of God and an ambassador of the covenant, it will be seen. As the Christian group dc Talk stated in their song *Jesus Freak*, "There ain't no disguising the truth." What you are will be made known because we either live *from* our heart, remaining true to who God has made us, or we will live *for* our heart, protecting it with smoke and mirrors, and the façade will eventually fall.

Likewise, Jesus went on to say that one does not light a lamp and hide it under a bowl. The lamp was to give light so that people could see their way around. You were redeemed for a reason and God put his light of truth in you for a purpose. We cannot fulfill that purpose if we are hidden away to tend our private life of faith. As I said before, your relationship with God is personal. Your walk of faith cannot be.

Had the apostle Paul kept his life of faith private, we would never have realized the impact his life could have. Paul's transformation moved him from a man who hid in religious zeal and hatred to a man who would write to the church in Thessalonica, "We loved you so much that we were delighted to share with you not only the gospel of God *but our lives as well,* because you had become so dear to us" (1 Thessalonians 2:8 – emphasis mine). Paul relied on neither a life quietly lived nor the spoken word, but both. The message of God was such a part of who he was that it came out in his speech and his actions. He invested himself in these people so they could hear and experience the truth of God. His public investment paid great dividends.

To take God's gift of salvation, light, and purpose and go our own way with it by keeping it to ourselves is to sin. It is written, "Anyone, then, who knows the good they ought to do and does not to it, to them it is sin" (James 4:17). We are also admonished "not to

receive God's grace in vain" (2 Corinthians 6:1), that is, to no end
or with no result. If we are able to remain unmoved to action by the
grace of God, then we have not really experienced it.

—

For the follower of Jesus Christ, compromise is not an option.
To be effective, we must remain true to who we are in Christ and to
the message we have been given. This does not mean that unless we
are perfect in word, thought, attitude, and deed that we are useless.
To the contrary, the covenant of God is one of restoration. What
better way to declare God's grace than to be faithful in our failures?
The biggest mistake we can make is to assume that the spirit of the
law — both its commands and its consequences — does not apply
to us. We are both bound to its holy standard, and recipients of its
grace.

Grace is not given in order to make your life easier or to afford
you an out. It is not an excuse to do the bare minimum. Grace is
meant to compel you to give your all. Jesus said that he did not
come to do away with the Law and the Prophets and the regulations
therein, but to fulfill them and make them complete. In fact, as
Jesus taught at the Sermon on the Mount, he often took the Law
and raised the standard! "You have heard it said, 'Do not commit
adultery.' But I tell you that anyone who looks at a woman lustfully
has already committed adultery with her in his heart" (Matthew
5:27-28). We often think that in Jesus, things get easier, that we are
no longer bound to obedience. Nothing could be further from the
truth. We are called to a persistent integrity.

If we are called to be ambassadors of the gospel of Jesus Christ,
then we can severely hinder that message and rob the gospel of its
power through our compromises. The grace of God is not a license
to sin. We cannot make disobedience an option. It is easy to use
grace as a safety net, allowing that option to go our own way or
let ourselves slide here or there. That willingness to give the devil a
foothold declares to the world that God is insufficient or that your
faith is a crutch. Faith half-lived can do greater damage to the cause
of Christ than it can good.

When I had been called to serve as pastor to Faith Community Church, my wife and I had been members of that congregation for ten years. We had seen a steady decline in attendance which also affected the budget. Slowly over those ten years the church transitioned from being proactive, to maintaining, and then to neglect. The buildings and the ministries began to deteriorate to the point that there was worry that we would have to close our doors.

Once called to serve the church, I took time to take a fresh look at who and where we were. Things were beginning to change, as they do when something new happens. We were beginning to see signs of life among our fellowship again. One Sunday, I stood before the congregation and told them that God was beginning to do some exciting things among us. We want to be able to tell those around us that God is alive in this place, but to look at the building the message it sends is that we are dead and rotting. We need to address these issues and bring the building back up to standard if we are to be effective in spreading the word that God is moving here.

Like our church, our lives can begin a downward spiral to death through one small compromise after another. Thriving becomes surviving, which becomes doubt and fear, which leads to despair. At that point, the enemy has effectively taken you out. A foothold does not have to be big. Rock climbers can support their entire body weight on a foothold no bigger than a pencil eraser. It doesn't take much.

A faithful and effective ambassador of the Kingdom is passionate about the gospel and his mission. They maintain an unbending, narrow integrity for the sake of God and his message.

> "In everything set them an example by doing what is good. In your teaching show integrity, seriousness and soundness of speech that cannot be condemned, so that those who oppose you may be ashamed because they have nothing bad to say about us."
> ~ Titus 2:7-8

With your desire to know God, a willingness to trust him, a healthy perspective, motivation, and passion, and when you develop your personal influence and begin to make a public investment, you can change the world. Guard your heart and your witness with a persistent integrity that relentlessly seeks to please God and represent him well.

—

One of the great struggles in the church is the concept of being in this world without being a part of this world. We grasp the theory, but it is the practice of it that becomes difficult. We have a tendency to bring with us all our upbringing and the trappings of our culture, we re-label it with Christian lingo and try to pass it off as kingdom living. We have a worldly view of success as we try to climb the ladder of ministry, and we still measure success by numbers, and numbers become our pride and our goal.

We have spent our entire lives — some longer than others — steeped in the world's culture, influenced by the world's thinking and desires, and motivated by what the world has to offer. We have been living in an economy of self for so long that it comes naturally to put self first. We have been circulating a currency of fear for so long that we jump to defend self and pursue what we determine to be good rather than confess our sin and seek God's best.

When God calls us out of the world and into the kingdom there is a radical transformation that happens. We become a new creation. Not a new version of the old you, but a totally new creation altogether. More than the language we use needs to change. We become different in the way we think and process information. Our motives are all new, and our hopes rest, not in our abilities or accomplishments, but in who God is and what God is doing and has done.

This economy of self, as we have already explored, is going bankrupt. In order to salvage our lives, individually and corporately, we must make an economic shift to a kingdom economy. This is not a loan modification or a refinance of existing debts and liabilities, but total abandonment of the old system to a completely new system.

This exchange follows the realization of our brokenness and need. When we come to face the reality that we are merely dirt and that our value and purpose comes from God, we become more willing to lay down our worthless trappings, move aside our self-made stumbling blocks, and follow where he leads. It sounds simple, and it really is, but it is not easy.

Remember, this exchange, this transformation, is a process. Don't allow yourself to get discouraged and overwhelmed by the big picture; just be faithful with the next step. Trust God with the big picture. Each small step in the process will make a significant difference in your life, and as you invest in others, as you are able and have opportunity, you will find yourself feeding this kingdom economy. As that economy begins to gain momentum, others will want a piece of the action. That is when we see the greatest dividends, what the Bible calls the "Treasure of heaven."

CHAPTER 5

FEEDING THE ECONOMY

Feeding the Economy

―

*"Command those who are rich in this present world not
to be arrogant nor to put their hope in wealth, which is so
uncertain, but to put their hope in God, who richly provides
us with everything for our enjoyment. Command them to do
good, to be rich in good deeds, and to be generous and willing
to share."*
~ 1 Timothy 6:17-18

God's work seldom appears linear. There is no definitive beginning and ending point; rather, it is cyclic. This is certainly true with the work he has begun in us. We are not called, take a few steps, and are then done. Just as the earth's orbit is a cycle, the seasons are a cycle, and life in general — the circle of life, as it were — is a cycle, so your spiritual development and kingdom investments are a cycle.

Think of it in terms of a CD or bond. You enter that cycle when you make an initial investment, say for retirement or college. As that investment matures, it grows through interest. When the deposit is matured, that initial investment should be re-invested in another CD or bond in order to keep growing. If ever you break that cycle, the money ceases to grow, probably gets spent, and yields no profit down the road. You have to keep investing for that initial investment to serve its purpose.

In the same way, God has made that initial investment for you. In the death of Christ your debt was paid, and by his resurrection you were given a life-line, and the presence of his Holy Spirit in your life serves as a deposit — a promise and assurance. Now it is up to you to continue rolling over, or re-investing, what God has given you in order for the initial investment to serve its purpose. As you continue to invest and re-invest, you are feeding the economy of the kingdom, and others will be drawn to enter the same process.

Marketing is a difficult job, particularly for a new product. Life in Christ is totally unlike anything we have known. You are God's marketing strategy. Through what people see in you they will experience the value of his "product." In the beginning, before the value of a product is really known, the idea is to keep the risk low. Remember, our society bases its decisions on fear. Remove that barrier by keeping the demands — or risks — at a minimum and people are more likely to give it a try.

God works in much the same way. When Jesus gave his Great Commission to his followers, he implemented a cycle that was meant to build trust, confidence, and momentum by starting with simple, low-risk investments and moving to higher-risk, higher-yield investments down the road.

> "All authority in heaven and on earth has been given to me. Therefore go and make disciples of all nations, baptizing them in the name of the Father and of the Son and of the Holy Spirit, and teaching them to obey everything I have commanded you. And surely I am with you always, to the very end of the age."
>
> ~ Matthew 28:18-20

It is important to be able to look back on your spiritual portfolio — your past investments. Therefore, the process begins with baptism. Baptism is not essential for salvation — otherwise Jesus lied to the thief on the cross who was promised Paradise but was never baptized.

Baptism is indicative of salvation. When we receive God's mercy and grace and surrender our lives to him, we follow in baptism as our first step of obedience and a declaration to those who witness it that we are a new creation in Christ, "Buried with him through baptism into death in order that, just as Christ was raised from the dead through the glory of the Father, we too may live a new life" (Romans 6:4). The lost who witness your baptism receive a testimony of God's life changing gospel. The saints who witness receive a testimony of the new birth of another brother or sister in Christ, and you experience a ceremony that serves as a spiritual marker for you to reflect on and remember what God has done for you.

Spiritual markers, such as baptism, will prove invaluable in your cycle of development and growth. We suffer from short-term memory and live by the credo, "What have you done for me lately?" To overcome the fear and doubt provided through our short-term memory, we need to be able to reflect on past investments — both those God has made in us and those we have made in others. Reflecting on how God has blessed you, and blessed others through you, will serve to encourage you and prepare you for the next steps you will be led to take. Every victory and failure is used to lead you along your journey of faith and prepare you for greater things yet to come.

Your baptism is, in many ways, your right of passage into the community of faith. Christ's blood is your passage into the kingdom, but through the common ground of "one baptism" (Ephesians 4:4-6), you are brought into fellowship with the saints who have come before you — you are made a part of a great whole and purpose. This is the very first investment after that initial deposit: plug in to the body.

Within the context of authentic Christian fellowship, you will be encouraged, challenged, and equipped. Here, particularly in the early years of your spiritual growth, you will receive more than you give. If it is a healthy community, you will be built up in your faith and encouraged in your walk. Those who are more mature will walk with you and invest in you. Make note of those people, of what they gave you, and how God used them to change you. Spend time recalling and celebrating God's faithfulness along your journey of faith. You can never give him too much credit. When you face challenges later on, it will help to recall those past investments. Like when your stocks struggle, you can look back on the annual report and reflect on its past earnings and (hopefully) find comfort for the future.

> "Therefore, I urge you, brothers, in view of God's mercy, to offer your bodies as living sacrifices, holy and pleasing to God – this is your spiritual act of worship. Do not conform any longer to the pattern of this world, but be transformed by the renewing of your mind. Then you will be able to test and approve what God's will is – his good, pleasing and perfect will.
>
> For by the grace given me I say to every one of you: Do not think of yourself more highly than you ought, but rather think of yourself with sober judgment, in accordance with the measure of faith God has given you. Just as each of us has one body with many members, and these members do not all have the same function, so in Christ we who are many form one body, and each member belongs to all the others."
>
> ~ Romans 12:1-5

We are given here a beautiful picture of God's initial investment and the very simple first step. We can also see the nature of the cycle. As we discussed, it requires humility to see yourself as broken and needy and to receive God's salvation. It takes another level of humility to see yourself as, not the main attraction, but rather a part of a whole. Finding a church body that you can connect with is personal, but also very important. We cannot thrive on our own. We need people who will pour into us and who we can pour in to. It is these Christ-centered, faith-filled investments we must remember and reflect on, not the fear-driven, failed investments of self.

Being a part of a church community is a two-way street. As you connect with the body, you will also have opportunity to invest in others as well. Remember back to our pond. In order to be filled it needs inlets: those people, ministries, or events that pour into us — that invest in us. Yet to remain fresh and useful, to have living (or moving) water, we also need outlets. We need to make investments, or we get scummy and become useless, yet we cannot make good investments apart from God's work in our lives. We need to be filled and to pour out.

> "We have different gifts, according to the grace given us. If a man's gift is prophesying, let him use it in proportion to his faith. If it is serving, let him serve; if it is teaching, let him teach; if it is encouraging, let him encourage; if it is contributing to the needs of others, let him give generously; if it is leadership, let him govern diligently; if it is showing mercy, let him do it cheerfully.
>
> Love must be sincere. Hate what is evil; cling to what is good. Be devoted to one another in brotherly love. Honor one another above yourselves. Never be lacking in zeal, but keeping your spiritual fervor, serving the Lord. Be joyful in hope, patient in affliction, faithful in prayer. Share with God's people who are in need. Practice hospitality."
>
> ~ Romans 12:6-13

This begins the thrust of the issue. If you are simply attending church, you are wasting your time. The Christian life is not about religion. Religion is merely involved as a means of expressing our love for, gratitude toward, and devotion to God. Sunday morning church attendance is the party. The Christian life is lived between Sundays. We will often play church because it makes us feel safe. It serves as a bandage for our wounded heart or a mask for our guilt

— just another way of hiding away our brokenness and hurt. That is not saving faith. It is idolatry.

Once baptized, the command of our Lord is to "teach them to obey everything I have commanded you." As the apostle Paul reiterated, "Work out your salvation with fear and trembling" (Philippians 2:12). In other words still, learn about faith, the kingdom, your place in it, and how to function as a part of it. "Now you are the body of Christ, and each one of you is a part of it" (1 Corinthians 12:27). You are a part of the body of Christ — the church. You have a God-ordained function and purpose. Your responsibility is simply to make the most of the opportunities you are given to invest yourself by discovering and using your resources and gifting, your faith and love.

We cannot make the investments we are called to as managers of God's gifts unless we have a right relationship with God through faith. In the middle of the above passage, Paul writes that "Love must be sincere." That love for God, and love for others, must be real. If it is not, what we are will eventually be shown through our collapse. In fact, literally, the Greek says, "(Let) love (be) undisguised/unassumed." It must be authentic, but also expressed. We cannot assume love. Love must be demonstrated through active participation in, and service to, the body.

In most English translations, these beginning admonitions are presented passively. "If his gift is…let him…" In the original language, there is a stronger exhortation. It may be better rendered, "If your gift is teaching, teach!" These are the entry-level investments we are expected to make, and they are relatively low-risk.

We often find safety and strength in numbers. It is far easier to stand for your beliefs when you are hidden among a crowd of like-minded people. It's a different story when you are one person among many from the other camp. If we cannot use our gifts, talents, and abilities among those who have committed to the same journey of faith as we have, then we will never do so. Granted, every church has its posers and hypocrites. In fact, every group does whether Christian or secular. Hopefully, your fellowship is one who will support and encourage authentic faith and correct and rebuke the posers.

There is no such thing as a perfect church. From the very beginning there was bickering among the twelve disciples. Most of the New Testament is letters from Paul to various churches addressing issues they were having among them. It would be great if we didn't have tension within the body of Christ. In fact, the Jehovah's Witness and Mormon faiths have both condemned Christendom as an apostate church because of the differences between orthodox denominations (as have some churches of those orthodox denominations). They have drawn a line in the theological sand and said, each of them, "You're either on our side, or you are outside." Naturally, we all want to be "in," not "out," so we are inclined to take the clearly outlined and uniform doctrine and the ultimatum. The problem is that minor, non-essential issues, like the shape of the cross, become definitive in determining one's salvation status and we put ourselves in God's place of judgment over issues of religion or interpretation. The other problem is that the people are intimidated (through…fear) into accepting these teachings and are rebuked for asking important questions, thus stunting authentic spiritual growth.

The truth is, different denominations actually have unity on the essential issues: that, though we differ on minor points, we are united in the faith under one Lord, and that we grow through adversity. "As iron sharpens iron, so one man sharpens another" (Proverbs 27:17). Sometimes, as iron sharpens iron, sparks fly. Do not let this frighten you, sour your spirit, or discourage you from engaging. These momentary difficulties and struggles, when we persevere, will make us stronger and draw us closer together. When the stock market drops one day, you don't just bail out. You know that there will be ups and downs, but that the payoff is in the long haul. The same trend applies here.

Your service to the body is beneficial — significant — in more ways than one. Through your commitment and service, you protect the unity of the church, advance the witness of the church, and nurture the church causing it to strengthen and grow.

"Be completely humble and gentle; be patient, bearing with one another in love. Make every effort to keep the unity of the Spirit through the bond of peace. There is only one body and one Spirit – just as you were called to one hope when you were called – one Lord, one faith, one baptism; one God and Father of all, who is over all, through all, and in all.

But to each one of us grace has been given as Christ apportioned it...It was he who gave some to be apostles, some to be prophets, some to be evangelists, and some to be pastors and teachers, to prepare God's people for works of service, so that the body of Christ may be built up until we all reach unity in the faith and in the knowledge of the Son of God and become mature, attaining to the whole measure of the fullness of Christ."

~ Ephesians 4:2-7, 11-13

You are a small, but important, part of the big picture. It is God who assembles his body, and you have a job to do, investments to make. Without your investments, your fellowship is incomplete and paints an incomplete picture of the kingdom of God. These low-risk investments in your brothers and sisters in Christ are meant to make the body whole — to make each other whole, and to train and equip you to make bigger, higher-risk investments down the road. Stay committed; stay invested; stay involved.

—

What we call the Great Commission is a cycle, a process. At our fellowship we communicate that through our vision as "Bringing people to God, Building people of God, and Serving people for God." The "bringing" aspect is making disciples and baptizing them into the fellowship. We provide opportunities for people to encounter God either for the first time, or at a deeper level, through worship, outreach events, and personal relationships.

Our "building" phase of the journey is teaching people the commands of our Lord Jesus and helping them figure out what obedience to those commands looks like. Our Sunday school, small group meetings, and discipling relationships facilitate this.

You may ask, "Where is the serving?" This is the loop. From teaching, the cycle goes back to the beginning, to "Go, therefore." In going we meet people at their felt needs — their fears and desires — in order to introduce them to Christ, his love, and his desire for them. These investments made outside the safety of our community of faith are high-risk investments. There is no guarantee of a return at all, let alone a good return. The high-risk investments are the ones that cost the most and promise the least. Yet, God commands us to make these investments. No excuses.

> "Bless those who persecute you; bless and do not curse. Rejoice with those who rejoice; mourn with those who mourn. Live in harmony with one another. Do not be proud, but be willing to associate with people of low position. Do not be conceited.
>
> Do not repay anyone evil for evil. Be careful to do what is right in the eyes of everybody. If it is possible, as far as it depends on you, live at peace with everyone. Do not take revenge, my friends, but leave room for God's wrath, for it is written: 'It is mine to avenge; I will repay,' says the Lord. On the contrary: 'If your enemy is hungry, feed him; if he is thirsty, give him something to drink. In doing this, you will heap burning coals on his head.'
>
> Do not be overcome by evil, but overcome evil with good."
>
> ~ Romans 12:14-21

First, the "burning coals" are a reference to shame, not a concession to "kill them with kindness." That is a motive from the economy of self.

What this passage is saying is that we need to engage those who may resent us for it. The truth is, we will never really know where a person stands or what their response will be until we engage them, but we will never impact our world for Christ, never affect change, never be "salt and light," if we keep our life of faith — and the message contained therein — in house. We have to take it outside.

We can talk the Christian game, recite scripture, and debate biblical principles and theology all we want. It will never have an impact unless it is experienced. The world will not, it cannot, do this for itself. Those who walk in darkness need the light brought to them. "This is the verdict: Light has come into the world, but men loved darkness instead of light because their deeds were evil. Everyone who does evil hates the light, and will not come into the light *for fear that his deeds will be exposed*" (John 3:19-20, emphasis mine).

This fear is what fuels the flames of persecution. Human pride seeks to protect itself; therefore, it will attack, socially, emotionally, morally, or physically, that which brings conviction. Persecution is an indicator that you are getting through on some level. This is when love must be both sincere and unassumed.

Love will never be proved if it is not demonstrated in adversity. The love of Christ endured rejection, betrayal, false accusation, abuse, ridicule, mockery, and even death. That is the standard. That is the love that has been deposited into your spiritual account, and it is the love from which you must live, and give. As Jesus said, "You have heard it said, 'Love your neighbor and hate your enemy.' But I tell you: Love your enemies and pray for those who persecute you, that you may be sons of your Father in heaven" (Matthew 5:43-45). Some things, we do not have to pray about. High-risk investments are the obligation of all God's children as we "love our enemies" from the love Christ has poured into us.

It is this indiscriminating love that will feed the kingdom economy and cause it to grow. It is in living this way that others are drawn in and a difference is made. Some degree of fear will always be present in our lives. It is a God-given emotion that makes us cautious. But if fear is what we base our decisions on, it is here that we will disconnect and fail. We cannot offer love or respond with an attitude of love to those who wish us ill or persecute us if we do not know God and trust him. This is the reason for the cycle: to continually prepare you for greater and greater things. We cannot remain in the small things, or our lives will remain small, and our impact will be small (if we have an impact at all).

> "Who is going to harm you if you are eager to do good? But even if you should suffer for what is right, you are blessed. 'Do not fear what they fear; do not be frightened.' But in your hearts set Christ apart as Lord. Always be prepared to give an answer to everyone who asks you to give the reason for the hope that you have. But do this with gentleness and respect, keeping a clear conscience, so that those who speak maliciously against your good behavior in Christ may be ashamed of their slander. It is better, if it is God's will, to suffer for doing good than for doing evil."
>
> ~ 1 Peter 3:13-17

The heart of the issue is that it is your persistent, consistent witness — your integrity — that will be used by God to convict hearts, to break up that hard soil to allow the seed of the gospel to be planted. Again, this is not about perfection. It is about consistency. Be consistent in your desire to please God, and, should you stumble or fall, remain consistent in your willingness to confess and repent and move on in the grace of God.

Well-known author Lee Strobel tells a story about an outreach event he attended at his church. One member of the community came with a bone to pick and what Lee thought would be a normal conversation developed into a heated argument. This man would challenge the faith and Lee would passionately defend it. It got so heated, however, that event security broke it up and escorted the man outside. Lee felt terrible about having nearly gone to blows with this man and figured he had ruined the opportunity to plant a seed.

It was some time later when Lee was able, again, to meet this same man who was surprisingly grateful for the encounter. Long had he searched for someone who would passionately defend what they claimed to be immutable truths. Lee's consistent and passionate stand on the truths of God touched this man's heart. I do not believe the man came to faith that day, but the seed of the gospel had broken through his calloused heart.

You too can have such an effect. The beauty of God's plan and process is that sometimes you will get to see the fruition of your witness and efforts, but most of the time, you will not. This means that there will be times where you are disappointed because you were hoping that your efforts would have been the ones to bear fruit. Other times you will be surprised because you were sure you blew it or missed something. This is where we need to trust that God is in control and has a plan, remain faithful to be who we are, and live the life we are called to in Christ.

—

Shortly after our financial crisis, early in our marriage, my wife and I came to the conclusion that the way we were doing things wasn't working. Our method of financial management was getting us into more and more trouble. Sure, we could hide the reality of it from others and appear stable, but in reality, we were sinking fast.

It is times like this that a budget can be very helpful. It lays out what you have to work with and where it needs to go. By implementing a budget, we were able to develop a spending (and savings) plan that would be stable, and even prosperous.

Once we implemented this budget process and spending plan, we had to stick to it before we would see results. It began with small steps: paying off smaller debts first and then bigger ones as we had more money to work with. Eventually, we were able to buy our first home, replace the car that had died…again, and establish a savings account — which was foreign to us.

God's process of bailing you out of your bankrupt economy of self is much the same. First, you have to identify the problem. Things are not what they were meant to be. Your natural longing for more is a first indication of that.

The next step is to shore up your debt. As we saw in the Beatitudes, we do this as we take an honest look at ourselves and God and the life we live. We need to realize that we cannot save ourselves and that we need what only God can offer.

As we grow and learn through experience who God is, we grow to trust him, and love him, and desire more of him in our lives — we hunger and thirst for him. To come to this place it requires consistent decisions to acknowledge and trust him. The more opportunities we give God to earn our trust, the faster that relationship will grow and the faster we will see ourselves develop. Fear gives way to faith and God's power is revealed to us and through us.

Self-improvement is not the end though. We are a part of a bigger picture. God intends for you to engage the church and the world around you. Beginning with safer, low-risk investments and moving to higher-risk, higher-yield investments, God will use you to begin to change the world.

You might be tempted to think that this is the end of the process, but nothing could be further from the truth. Remember, God's work is a cycle that will continue in you "until the day of Christ Jesus" (Philippians 1:6). Just when you think you are all shored up, God will break through again and reveal areas of your life that are not what they ought to be. It is here that your cycle begins anew.

It is also tempting to think that there is too much work to be done and become discouraged. Because of the cyclic nature of God's work, he will begin small, with just your next step, and then lead you along from there. He wants you to succeed, for in this he is glorified; through this others can also see who he is.

My prayer for you, the reader, is that God would show you your next step. Maybe you have professed a belief in God and the Lord Jesus, but your life is still governed by your fears. Perhaps you have grown content and are feeling the need to engage others and pour out from that which you have been given. It may be that you have never heard this before and that you viewed the Christian life through the criticism of others, never knowing that there is a better, more stable way to live. There is hope no matter what station you find yourself in. Like most debt consolidators, there is no one God can't help. Unlike those fiscal snake-oil salesmen, this is no scam.

I pray that you will find enough courage to take that first baby step of trust. "Taste and see that the LORD is good" (Psalm 34:8). Step away from your safety nets and the façade of security and take a step toward God. Let your fear be an indicator that change is on the horizon, but allow faith and hope to guide your decisions.

Your money is no good here. It is time to exchange it and be free.

9 781449 717254